Mesibov, Schopler, and TEACCH

If You Can Find It Elsewhere, You Won't Find It Here

If you can find it with Google or it is described in articles or books, you probably won't find it in this book. Why would you need to?

In this book you will find stories, opinions, ideas, and anecdotes based on the personal experiences of professionals, people with autism spectrum disorder (ASD), and parents of people with ASD, based on what they've learned between the 1960s and the present.

With this book you will be able to trace the history of autism research and practices as told by the people who were there.

Mesibov, Schopler, and TEACCH

Changing the World for Parents,
and People with Autism

By

Don Mesibov

with

Eighty-Three Coauthors

Cover photo:
September 14, 2010: Dr. Masami Sasaki is presented with The Eric Schopler Lifetime Achievement Award by Dr. Gary Mesibov, former Director of the TEACCH program.

ISBN: 9798840583487

About The Author

Don Mesibov is the author or coauthor of five books, four of which are focused on the education field. His most recent, published this past June, is entitled, "Helping Students Take Control of Their Own Learning." A memoir, published in 2010, focused on the last nine months of his mother's life when, in the advanced stages of Alzheimer's, Don, and his wife Susan and their two daughters, brought her to live with them; their son, out of the nest, frequently visited.

Upon graduation from Boston University with a degree in communications/public relations, Don went to work at the checkout counter of the Star Market in Brookline, Massachusetts. "I wanted to raise money to buy an overnight summer camp," he explained, "but I had no funds of my own; so I earned enough at the super market to live on and travelled weekends trying to locate investors. Although I ultimately failed to raise sufficient funding, the experience getting to know people in a different context has served me well through life."

Don currently works as an educational consultant, training teachers to actively engage students in the learning process. During a varied career he has worked as a door-to-door encyclopedia salesman; a summer camp counselor, then athletic director; a child-care counselor at a school for children with special needs; a reporter, then editor, of a weekly newspaper; a teachers' union labor relations specialist; and for the past 28 years he has been director of The Institute for Learning Centered Education, an organization he founded.

Don is an avid gardener with 175 flower gardens at his home in Potsdam, New York, near the Canadian border. His wife Susan tends to nine raised beds which provide food for the summer as well as products that can be frozen and partaken during the long, cold Potsdam winters. "Our father, and grandfather (mine and Gary's), each died of heart attacks at the age of 52, so I have always been aware of the need to exercise. When I was younger," Don continues, "I would run a lot, but I found running in circles to be exceedingly boring. However, I can get out in the gardens at 8 am and still be working, and enjoying it, when Susan yells from the house, "Don't you know it's getting dark?"

The author and his wife Susan

Books by author Don Mesibov

Helping students Take Control of their Own Learning – 279 Learner-Centered, Social Emotional Strategies for Teachers (Mesibov and Drmacich, 2022, Routledge, Taylor and Frances Group)

Appreciating Mom through The Lens of Alzheimer's – A Care Giver's Story (Mesibov, 2014, Create Space)

Captivating Classes with Constructivism (Flynn, Mesibov, Vermette, Smith, 2013, Rainmaker Education)

Applying Standards-Based Constructivism: A Two-Step Guide for Motivating Elementary Students (Flynn, Mesibov, Vermette, Smith, 2004, Eye on Education)

Applying Standards-Based Constructivism: A Two-Step Guide for Motivating Middle and High School Students (Flynn, Mesibov, Vermette, Smith, 2004, Eye on Education)

A Letter to the President

Dear Mr. President:

No Child Left Behind was a Bush administration initiative that resulted in limited success at substantial financial expense. *Race to the Top* was an Obama administration initiative that similarly produced limited results at substantial financial expense.

Why not try something that will greatly improve the ability of our schools to address the educational needs of each student, and will require little or no financial expense? Use your bully pulpit to encourage educational institutions to focus on training teachers to create student-centered classrooms. These are classrooms in which teachers actively engage their students with visual, kinesthetic, and auditory approaches that students find relevant to their own lives and interests and, hence, motivating.

The key to improving our schools begins in the classroom. Strategies for teaching students with autism or other special needs, as well as high performing students who need to be challenged to think critically, are Best Practices for ALL students.

Respectfully submitted for your consideration,

Don Mesibov

Don Mesibov

Table of Contents

Credentials of Eighty-Three Coauthors

A Primer for Reading This Book

This book is based on eighty-three personal interviews, and contributors are often quoted more than once. One of the first times a person is quoted, the reader will find a brief description of that person's background. Whether the person's background is identified the first, second, or third time the person is quoted will depend on the context; however, you will be able to identify anyone quoted by referring to appendix A, where all who have contributed their reflections to this manuscript will be listed and identified.

By utilizing Appendix A, if someone is quoted on page 24 and then again on page 124, the reader will not have to remember what was written one hundred pages earlier nor scour the previous one hundred pages to recall the background of the person who is quoted.

People with Autism or Autistic People?

Among the eighty-three professionals, people with autism, and parents of autistic people with whom the author has spoken, there was disagreement about whether we should refer to "people with autism" or to "autistic people." Some feel strongly one way or the other, and some use the references interchangeably. In this manuscript the author has used whatever term was conveyed to him by the person being quoted or referenced.

Definition of Terms

For definitions of a few key terms such as TEACCH and Structured Teaching, see page 283.

Introduction

Were it not for my brother being overtaken by Alzheimer's, I probably would not have thought to write about his career as the go-to person in the world for more than forty years for information about autism, support, and training.

Since June 28, 1945, when Gary was born, we have had a close relationship and pride in each other's accomplishments without envy. The closest we might have come to conflict was when I tried to scare my younger brother in the darkness late at night with talk of ghosts in the closet and under his bed in the room we shared until he was six.

However, I knew little about Gary's work in the field of autism because when we spoke, it was about politics, sports, or family—"Was it chickens or ducklings Mom kept in a corner of the kitchen one winter?" We were both fanatical sports fans, although I was not good enough to make any of my school teams. Gary was catcher on the varsity baseball team, but his athletic career ended with his graduation from high school. My childhood idol was Jackie Robinson; Gary's was Willie Mays. A highlight of my life was a forty-minute interview I conducted with Robinson in 1962 as a reporter for WBUR, Boston University's radio station at the time. For Gary's seventieth birthday celebration, I smothered him with Willie Mays memorabilia.

According to our mother, were it not for me, my brother's name would be Bruce Mesibov instead of Gary Bruce Mesibov, as it reads on his birth certificate. I was a few months shy of my fourth birthday when my parents told me they intended to name him Bruce. "Oh, boy," I exclaimed, "I can call him Brucey-Goosey."

Because we rarely discussed our careers, all I really knew about Gary's work was that he was a pioneer in the field of autism, had cowritten ten books with his boss in the late 1900s, had traveled to Japan many times to conduct autism training, and enjoyed being an expert witness in court cases. I wanted to do something for Gary, and I decided a book about his career as a pioneer in the field would be what I could do best for him. It would be something to leave his children, daughters-in-law, and grandchildren.

It was October 2021, and I was ready to begin learning enough about Gary's career to write a book. Then the panic set in: Would I be able to uncover enough information for more than a five-page booklet? Would there be anyone around who worked with Gary before the year 2000? Was he enough of a pioneer to justify putting a focus on his contributions to the field of autism?

Gary's son, Todd, and his wife, Katie, put me in touch with Kathy Hearsey and Mary Beth Van Bourgondien, and I arranged to meet with them and Gary in his room at the assisted living facility where he resided. Both had worked at TEACCH with Gary starting in the late 1970s as graduate students and were still employed in important positions, Kathy as director of training, and Mary Beth as a TEACCH faculty member and clinician.

At the conclusion of a productive two-hour session, they suggested a few people I could contact. I immediately emailed these people and set up Zoom sessions with them, at the conclusion of which each suggested additional people for me to contact. Each time I held a Zoom with someone, that person would suggest others. Then I started receiving emails from people who said they had heard I was writing a book about Gary and would love to have the opportunity to speak with me.

At the time of this writing, I have personally held seventy-five Zoom discussions over a three-month period, each of at least an hour, most closer to two hours. Since some of my discussions were with spouses or families, I have actually held discussions about Gary, Eric Schopler, TEACCH, and autism with eighty-three people, all through Zoom meetings except for in-person meetings with three people. My zoom meetings have included people in Australia, Canada, Denmark, England, Germany, Japan, and Sweden and with others throughout the world, including the United States.

Just three TEACCH trainers, Lee Marcus, Kathy Hearsey, and Mary Beth Van Bourgondien, have offered training or presentations in more than twenty-nine countries on six continents and in twenty-five states and the District of Columbia. Consider that many other TEACCH trainers as well as Eric Schopler and Gary Mesibov have been to these same countries, states, and other locations around the world many times over, and the reach and impact of TEACCH comes into focus. Add to this the people in many countries who, after being trained by Gary and his colleagues, went on to train people in other countries.

The following are typical of responses I received when I would send an email introducing myself, my purpose, and my desire to set up a one-to-two-hour Zoom to discuss my brother's role in the field of autism:

- Viviane de Leon, Brazil, occupational therapist with master's and doctoral degrees in psychology: "Hello, Don; It will be an honor for me to talk with you about Gary. TEACCH has been my professional life in Brazil. The legacy of Dr. Mesibov and Dr. Schopler inspired all my professional life in the field of autism. And TEACCH helped so many families here in Brazil."
- Susan Moreno, Indiana, parent of a child with ASD, autism trainer, and resource provider: "I would love to Zoom with you. I have many wonderful stories about Gary, how he boosted my career, and how he impacted so many of us who are parents of loved ones on the spectrum."

- Kara Hume, TEACCH® certified advanced consultant and associate professor at University North Carolina (UNC) at Chapel Hill: "I would love to be part of this. Gary and TEACCH have been such a key part of my life and career. Thank you."

And finally this is an unsolicited email I received in mid-May, when I thought I had conducted my last Zoom interview and which led to four additional interviews and the addition of a chapter on Gary, autism, and the criminal justice system:

My name is Melissa Sreckovic (Michigan), and I heard you are writing a book about Gary and looking for stories about his reach, including his impact on graduate students, and about his work in the criminal justice system. I would love the opportunity to share my experiences with Gary for the book you are writing.

As a consequence of my many discussions, it rapidly became apparent to me that credit for the meaningful leaps in understanding autism since 1943, when Leo Kanner made his audiences familiar with the word "autism," to the present extends far beyond my brother. How can one downplay the significance of Eric Schopler, whose research refuted the theory of the "refrigerator mother" being responsible for autism in her children? Or the fact that Gary would not have given a thought to a career in autism were it not for Eric's tutelage and then partnership for thirty-three years? Before Gary came along to attain go-to recognition throughout the world, Eric had already become a celebrity in autism research in Japan, the United States, and other countries.

Also, Gary would be the first to acknowledge that his own impact was due to collaborations with the many TEACCH trainers, therapists, people with autism and their families, and other professionals who joined with him over the years to educate the world about autism. Recognizing how many people made their own selfless contributions to the support now available to people with autism not only does not diminish what Gary has contributed; it actually magnifies it. Gary has attracted a following among so many distinguished people in the field of autism that to list the books, articles and accolades attributed to them would require a book in itself—a rather thick book.

Many of the people I contacted spoke of Gary's exceptional listening skills, including Vickie Shea, a graduate of Vassar, who came to the University of North Carolina (UNC) in 1971 for its doctoral program and then began an internship with TEACCH in 1974, subsequently working in various capacities with TEACCH before starting her own practice. Vicki told me, "Gary could sit in a corner and just observe a single parent interacting with their child or observe an entire group. Sometimes we thought of this as an ant farm: Gary liked to look and observe before diving in. His ability to go from small details to the larger picture was intellectually wonderful."

Perhaps Gary honed his listening skills during the more than three years after I left the nest to go to Lehigh University for a year and then Boston University. Gary often mentioned how he would sit in the corner listening as our mother, our aunt, and sometimes our grandmother would sit around talking about us, forgetting Gary was within earshot. He would hear about the joys, heartaches, and challenges of raising us as children and supporting and communicating with us as young adults. He learned that all he had to do was remain silent and let them forget he was overhearing in order to discover what our cousins Gail and Fred and I would never hear.

What I hope the reader will find different and interesting about this book is that instead of being the sole author, I have become an editor of recollections, stories, anecdotes, and histories as told by the people in the trenches. My story has become their stories, stories told to help us all understand more about the culture of autism, because as Matthew Hardie, a thirty-five-year-old man with autism, said to me from his home in England, "The problem is not those of us with autism; the problem is the perceptions of other people."

Chapter One

Here's to the Children Who Don't Quite Fit

Here's to the children who don't quite fit
Who run around aimlessly when all the others sit
Who look at the world through eyes unique
And into their souls you'd love to peek
To see just what magic makes them tick
When they look at a tree and call it a stick

Here's to the teens who will not abide
By life's set rules that they push aside
As they rock back and forth in their own special world
While grown-ups grow frustrated with lips tightly curled
Then bursts of brilliance they reveal as they race
While tears of love roll down a parent's face
Expectations often missed but still they yearn
Wondering today what skills they will learn

We hope for the ones who don't quite fit the mold
That the world will be kind as they grow old
We know that the bullies will play their cruel game

Reality is, cruelty sometimes brings shame
But optimism lives in each heart and mind
Of parents and professionals who continue to be kind

With a network of supporters shining bright as the sun
The ones who don't quite fit have already won
Nobody knows the future
So why pretend?
Let's celebrate their victories!
May they never end!!!
(Gary Shulman, MS Ed., August 24, 2021)

Gary Shulman was an advocate in New York City for parents of children with disabilities for over thirty years. During that time he worked with, provided workshops for, and advocated for a multitude of parents and foster parents caring for children with autism.

Chapter Two

A Collaboration Changed the World for People with Autism

Autism affects how people think.
Grayson Delisle, age twelve

Between them, Eric Schopler and Gary Mesibov changed understandings, strategies, and training in the field of autism around the world.

Eric:

- was largely responsible for refuting the prevalent theory in the 1960s that women known as "refrigerator mothers" were responsible for their children being autistic due to being cold and distant during the child-rearing years.
- insisted that parents be treated as partners of therapists rather than as the guilty ones.
- understood politics sufficiently to lead a lobbying movement that resulted in North Carolina becoming the first state in the nation to provide statewide funding for autism support services.

- traveled the world sharing his research and training with people in other states and countries to support people with ASD and their families.
- focused on support for children with autism and their families.

Gary:

- advised the King of Saudi Arabia about his grandson who had been diagnosed with autism.
- was sought after by a high-ranking Russian official who had scoured the world to find the best person to council him on autism.
- created a model for addressing the needs of autistic people and is credited by many with spreading this model throughout every continent except Antarctica.
- visited the United Kingdom sixty-two times, Japan forty times, and countless other countries from Australia to Singapore to conduct training and give presentations during his forty-four-year career.
- was treated like a rock star wherever he went; people gathered around him as if he were a member of the Beatles.
- focused on adolescents and adults with autism and their families.

Gary and Eric:

- cowrote ten books on autism between 1979 and 1999.
- promoted the idea of including people with ASD and their parents as partners of professionals in training sessions and in determining strategies for addressing the needs of people with autism and their families.

By 2005, the TEACCH program which Eric and Robert Reichler had founded in 1972, and Gary had helped nourish since 1973, had expanded to the point where Eric was able to say, it "has served thousands of individuals and families. . . . It now employs hundreds of staff with multi-disciplinary training."

If I said to you that for half a century, Gary Mesibov has been the go-to person across six continents for advice on and training in autism, it is understandable if your reaction would be, "Of course you think highly of him; Gary is your brother."

Well, I won't ask you to take my word for it. Come along with me as I share the journey I've taken over a period of several months, and see if you don't agree that Gary Mesibov, Eric Schopler, and their colleagues in Chapel Hill, North Carolina, and around the world through the TEACCH program have significantly—and in some ways, singularly—influenced understandings, strategies, and training in support of people with ASD, their families, and their teachers.

Chapter Three

The Journey from "Refrigerator Mothers" to the Present

Eric, Gary, and the TEACCH program are to the field of autism what Leonard Bernstein is to music, Isaac Newton and Marie Curie are to science, Rembrandt is to art, and Babe Ruth is to baseball.

Don Mesibov

Here is an abbreviated timeline of how the roles of Eric Schopler, Gary Mesibov, and the TEACCH program evolved to the present from Leo Kanner's description, in 1943, of "infantile autism," and Bruno Bettelheim's characterization of "refrigerator mothers" as the ones responsible for their children's autism.

1908: Psychiatrist Eugen Bleuler first uses the term "autism" to describe a subset of schizophrenic patients who were especially withdrawn and self-absorbed

1943: Leo Kanner, a child psychiatrist at Johns Hopkins University in Baltimore, Maryland, is credited with introducing the word "autism" into the professional literature. Kanner identified three areas of difficulty for people with autism: social isolation, abnormal communication, and insistence on repetitive, narrow routines.

1944: A German scientist named Hans Asperger describes a "milder" form of autism now known as Asperger's syndrome.

1963: Eric Schopler joins the faculty of UNC at Chapel Hill the same year that he attains his doctorate from the University of Chicago, where he had been an investigator and therapist.

Through his research, writings, and teaching, he would eventually confirm that autism is neurological, not psychological. He furthered the understanding that behavioral problems exhibited by people with ASD were not the result of intent or malice; behavioral problems were caused by the frustration of being in a world where one could not effectively communicate or understand what others were trying to convey.

1964: Bruno Bettelheim is hired to be the director of the Orthogenic School for Troubled Children at the University of Chicago as a residential treatment milieu for such children.

1967: Bettelheim, with an international reputation, gains widespread acceptance of the theory first described by Kanner several years earlier that children with behavioral and emotional disorders were not born that way and could be treated through extended psychoanalytic therapy and treatment. In his book *Empty Fortress: Infantile Autism and the Birth of the Self,* Bettelheim promotes the "refrigerator mother" misinformation that suggests that mothers cause children to have autism by being too cold and distant while raising their children.

Brenda Denzler was an editorial assistant to Eric Schopler at TEACCH for many years, and Brenda indicates, "There is a stone mother sculpture that Bettelheim had put in his institute's yard as a representation of the cold, uncaring mothers that caused autism."

Photo of the stone mother sculpture supplied by Brenda Denzler

1968: Schopler is instrumental in changing the perception of the "refrigerator mothers."

1970: Betsy Schopler, Eric's wife from 1953 to 1970, explained that a legislative breakfast attended by parents and their children with autism resulted in North Carolina being the first state to provide funding for autism services. Brenda Denzler refers to a key moment later in this chapter as "Grits and the Governor's Tie," when a child with autism spilled grits all over the lieutenant governor's tie, leading Eric to believe all hope was lost.

1971: The North Carolina State Legislature passes Senate Bill 383, "An Act to Establish a Special Program for the Training and Education of Children with Severe Learning, Communication and Behavior Disorders." This is the first piece of legislation in the United States to make a place for children with autism in the public schools instead of confining them to psychiatric centers, and it helps launch the TEACCH program the following year.

Schopler and Robert Reichler become founders and codirectors of *Treatment and Education of Autistic and Related Communication Handicapped Children* (TEACCH).

Robert Reichler

1973: Gary Mesibov enrolls at UNC to pursue postdoctoral work. He is mentored by Eric Schopler, and together, Eric, Gary, and the many TEACCH trainers who work with them provide the sparks that ignite a revolution in the field of autism throughout the world.

1976: Reichler takes a job in the state of Washington, and Schopler becomes sole director of TEACCH.

1977: Research on twins finds that autism is largely caused by genetics and biological differences in brain development—a theory Schopler had been promoting more than a decade earlier.

1978: Gary is hired in the role of director of adolescent and adult services and is now officially an assistant to Eric Schopler.

1979: Eric and Gary put on the first annual TEACCH conference in Greensboro, North Carolina (a tradition still happening forty-three years later).

1983: Gary becomes associate director to TEACCH. Eric and Gary coauthor and publish their first of ten books. It is based on the 1979 conference regarding autism in adolescents and adults with autism. This is the first of a series of books titled *Current Issues in Autism* and based on the theme of the yearly conferences. Often Eric and Gary would enlist others to write chapters for their books.

1985: Theo Peeters, a Belgian neurolinguist who specializes in autism spectrum disorder, travels to Chapel Hill, North Carolina to participate in TEACCH training. He then invites Gary to bring TEACCH trainers to

Belgium for a conference. Leaders from other European countries participate in the training in Belgium, and this begins a cycle of invitations to Eric, Gary, and their TEACCH trainers to come to their countries.

1986: TEACCH launches what is to become an annual event with four weeks of training in July; each week a different group comes to Chapel Hill from anywhere in the world. Kathy Hearsey says proudly, "This five-day hands-on training in a demonstration classroom was held in Chapel Hill, and it continued annually in North Carolina, both in July as well as in the fall and spring, until the start of the pandemic."

1988: Gary becomes co-director of TEACCH in 1988

1989: The Supported Employment (SE) program has its beginnings, designed by people Gary hired for this purpose.

1993: Eric retires, although he stays on as consultant; Gary takes over as Director of TEACCH

2006: Eric dies at age seventy-nine.

2009: Gary resigns as director of TEACCH but continues as a member of the faculty of UNC.

2011: Laura Klinger is hired to replace Gary.

2012: Gary retires from the faculty of UNC at Chapel Hill.

2018: Gary travels to England and Japan for his last trips away from Chapel Hill.

Thinking about the "refrigerator mother" theory and how so many professionals could allow it to go unchallenged for so long, the question arises: How could anyone give credence to a theory that mothers were responsible for children with autism? Didn't anyone question how one child in a family might have autism, and others raised by the same allegedly cold and distant parents didn't? Why did no one investigate the personalities and parenting practices of the mothers of children who were autistic?

John Donvan and Caren Zucker may provide the answer in their best-selling 2016 book, *In A Different Key*, (2016, page 74) in which they point out that at the time (the 1960s), "autism was such a rare diagnosis, and so little research had been done on it, that few medical doctors knew anything about it or had even heard of it." The authors point out that by 1966,

> The medical literature contained references to hundreds more children who…shared the behaviors that Kanner had linked together. Still, despite the mounting numbers, almost no sustained effort was being made to scientifically explore autism's essential nature. In part, this was because scientists viewed the condition as too rare to justify much attention. The bigger factor, however, was psychiatry's blanket certainty that it already knew why some children had autism and others did not. The verdict, "Autism was caused by mothers not loving their children enough."

(Editor's note: Our older daughter, Marli, added a dimension to the explanation of why researchers were content to not challenge the "refrigerator mothers" theory: "Dad," she told me, "another way to put this is that the researchers' 'blanket certainty' was due to the patriarchy.")

Chapter Four

What Eric, Gary, and the TEACCH Program Have Set in Motion

> Eric's father had been a successful attorney when Hitler decreed those Jewish professionals had to limit their practice to clients who were Jewish.
>
> Betsy Schopler

In this chapter we'll take a look at some of the highlights of the work on autism accomplished by Eric, Gary, TEACCH trainers, and so many others between the 1960s and the present.

Eric Schopler had arrived at UNC in 1964 and had already been challenging the prevailing theories of the causes of autism when Gary had come, ten years later, for its postdoctoral program. Years later, reflecting on Bettelheim's articulation of the theory of "refrigerator mothers," Eric had written:

My interest in autism first took shape while I was in graduate school at the University of Chicago when a psychology professor by the name of Bruno Bettelheim shared his excitement about the

University Orthogenic School he had taken over. He said that he was solving the puzzle of the 'mental illness' of autism by removing affected children from their parents' home and keeping them as long as possible at his residential school.

Bettelheim taught the counselors at the school that emotionally cold parents had produced the autistic features in their children through their unconscious feelings of hostility and rejection. These parents were, he said, like concentration camp guards, and the children were the victims, just as he himself had been a concentration camp victim in Nazi Germany"

When I read about Bettelheim I thought to myself, "Can one imagine what it must have been like for a mother who was just becoming aware that her child had this whatever it was, constantly threw tantrums, and couldn't effectively communicate and to be told authoritatively that she was the cause?" (The TEACCH Approach to Autism Spectrum Disorders, Mesibov, Gary B., Shea, Victoria, Schopler Eric, 2005, Page 1. Also, information provided by Brenda Denzler based on interviews with Eric Schopler).

It is interesting to note that two of the most prominent people in the early days of researching the causes of autism had endured disillusioning experiences related to Nazi Germany but with completely different thoughts about their experiences as they relate to their work in the field of autism. Bettelheim had been in a concentration camp, hence his damning rhetoric comparing parents of children with ASD to Nazi guards.

According to Eric's first wife, Betsy (married 1953–1970),

Eric was eleven years old in 1938 when his father, Ernest Schopflocher, fled Germany. His father had been a successful attorney when Hitler decreed those Jewish professionals had to limit their practice to clients who were Jewish.

Still, Ernst intended to remain in Germany until a friend who was an SS guard advised him to leave the country. Initially, when Ernst was reluctant, the SS guard showed him a master plan for the Jews and that convinced the father to take Eric, his brother, who was eight, his sister, eighteen, and his wife to the United States. Fortunately, he had a brother in Milwaukee who paved the way for the family because in the 1930s it was a requirement that you have a relative in the United States in order to immigrate here.

The family experienced much of the antisemitism that existed in the United States at that time, as depicted in 1942's Academy-Award-winning film *Gentleman's Agreement*, where Gregory Peck portrayed a reporter who posed as being Jewish in order to learn firsthand about antisemitism.

When in 1960 Eric joined the faculty at the University of Chicago, which had many professors who were Jewish, he commented, "This is the time in my life when I am proudest of my Jewish heritage."

Ironically, on our first date, we went to a presentation at the Hillel and heard the Jewish lecturer tell us: "Antisemitism is your fault. You need to assimilate and stop being Jewish."

After working as a social worker in Rochester, New York prior to 1958, Eric then worked at a hospital in Rhode Island, where he came across a girl with autism, and he was fascinated by her. As a result he was inspired to go to the University of Chicago. In 1960, while still at the university, he took a part-time job working for Bruno Bettelheim. Eric stood up to Bettelheim to the point where Bettelheim invited him to meet and discuss.

The Cow Puzzle

In the early 1960's, in order to educate people about the differences in brain function that made people with autism unique, Eric began developing ideas for his dissertation. He utilized the cow puzzle to demonstrate how significantly different people with autism's learning styles can be from other people's. When a decade later Gary began stressing the importance of understanding what is in the brain of each individual person with autism *before* developing strategies to support them, it helped parents and professionals focus on not trying to design a one-size-fits-all approach to people with autism.

Here's the cow puzzle story as told by Eric during an interview Brenda conducted with him on December 17, 2001, in Carrboro, North Carolina, in Eric's TEACCH office:

The cow in the cow puzzle story, supplied by Brenda Denzler

In the 1960's I had worked up this dissertation proposal when I noticed that the kids were touching and smelling things more than they would use their distance receptors of vision and audition, and, so I thought, it would be neat to show that in a dissertation. Nobody's done that. And, uh, I worked out these little gadgets where I would compare visual interest with, uh, tactile interest for the same object. So, on the visual side I'd have, let's say, some puppets rotating on a disk. And on the tactile side I'd have the same puppets inside of a bag. They could only explore tactilely.

The Cow Puzzle

The cow puzzle is one of the things I used in my dissertation research to show that children with autism use near-receptor systems like touch over distance-receptor systems like vision. I had a neighbor draw a picture of a cow, and then I cut it into equal rectangular pieces so that you could only put it back together right by using visual cues. Then I made another puzzle with different, interconnecting shapes for all of the pieces, like a traditional puzzle. But when this one was put together, the visual image was scrambled.

Children who were not autistic had trouble with the scrambled puzzle but did well with the cow puzzle because they were using the visual images on the pieces as guides for putting them together. The autistic kids, though, paid less attention to the visual image and used their sense of touch to figure out how to fit the pieces together, so they had trouble with the cow puzzle but did the scrambled puzzle much faster than the other kids.

Betsy continues the story:

In 1964 Eric's brother (John) got him a job in Chapel Hill, and Eric secured a grant that allowed him to continue his work on autism. Because of his work, a few years later, parents of children with autism went from being the bad guys to being the good guys.

As demonstrated by the cow puzzle, Eric learned that people with ASD were good with neuroreceptors that were close by, but not good with receptors for distant sounds, hence they were not easily influenced by auditory messages. When his grant ran out, it became evident that UNC would not pick up the funding. At some point Eric did persuade UNC to provide some funding, and periodically, when the budget people would move to reduce his funding, Eric would threaten to take his work to Duke, and somehow the funding would not be reduced. Actually Eric was relaxed about funding over the years because of the results he was seeing. Whereas Bettelheim blamed mothers for their children with autism, Eric believed, "Parents are the solution, not the problem."

Tom Schopler, the youngest of Eric's and Betsy's three children, told me, "He was great with ideas; he left the details to others. He was good at letting people use their strengths."

An excellent example is how Eric utilized the strength of parent lobbying to lead to North Carolina's legislature becoming the first in the nation to approve state funding for research on and treatment of autism. This story is shared by Catherine Faherty, a TEACCH certified advanced consultant, who describes how a grant, awarded in 1968 became the steppingstone toward the creation of the TEACCH program:

> Eric, through a three-year Child Research Study grant, rented classrooms in three North Carolina public schools spanning the state from the west to the east. In this study, parents of the students volunteered in these three classrooms along with staff as they worked with the children and figured out how to teach them in what we might now say are autism-friendly ways. It was from this three-year experience in actual classrooms that the seeds of visually Structured Teaching began, eventually to be developed and known as TEACCH Structured Teaching.
>
> On the first day of our Asheville TEACCH Center training, this story about "How TEACCH started" would be told by the late Roger Cox who had been director of the Asheville and Greensboro TEACCH centers and then director of training for the TEACCH program. He would explain that funding from the three-year children's research grant was about to end in 1971, so Eric attended a meeting in Greensville with the parents of children with ASD who

had been supportive of his work, and he told them the money had run out, and he explained what he believed they had already accomplished. He encouraged parents to lobby with legislators by asking, "Wouldn't it be great to go to the legislators for funding?" but he let the parents work out the details and take it from there. Betty Camp and Mary Lou "Bobo" Warren then took the lead together with other parents, and the turning point was an annual legislative breakfast.

Ad for "Child Research" project supplied by Brenda Denzler

Andy Short, a clinical psychologist who worked for and consulted with TEACCH from 1983 through 2013, describes the breakfast,

Parents of children with autism brought their children with them, an unorthodox approach, and each legislator was seated at a table with a child with autism and a parent. The legislators saw the children with their eccentricities and their charm and quickly began to appreciate the special difficulties that these families faced. The outcome was funding for the first statewide approach for supporting families of people with autism and the creation of TEACCH.

Here is Eric's own recollection of that breakfast from a 2005 interview conducted by Brenda Denzler that Brenda titled "Grits and the Governor's Tie":

The legislator we needed most was the lieutenant governor because he is the speaker of the house, and he sets the agenda for new legislation. Mr. Taylor, the lieutenant governor, had not arrived, so we started without him. We only had about twenty-five minutes to do our presentation.

Mr. Taylor came in late and sat next to one of our toughest kids, not a place where we expected him to sit down. The child, George, reached over, picked up a handful of grits, and tried to feed the lieutenant governor. The grits went all over his tie and made a big mess. I thought, "Oh my Lord! This is the end of our effort." But it turned out the opposite because this politician recognized that the boy was trying to make a social overture, and he just didn't know how to do it. So instead of being put off by having his tie soiled, he got hooked on George, and the legislation was passed.

Because parents had such a major role in lobbying for passage of this bill, it even further reinforced the view of parents as collaborators. Previously parents had been seen as part of the problem. Now they were viewed as an essential part of the solution.

STATE OF NORTH CAROLINA
Department of State

I, THAD EURE, Secretary of State of the State of North Carolina, do hereby certify the following and hereto attached   FOUR   (4) sheets to be a true copy of   CHAPTER 1007   , 1971 Sessions Laws entitled

AN ACT TO ESTABLISH A SPECIAL PROGRAM FOR THE TRAINING AND EDUCATION OF CHILDREN WITH SEVERE LEARNING, COMMUNICATION AND BEHAVIOR DISORDERS.

ratified on the 20th day of   July   , 19 71 , by

The General Assembly of North Carolina

the original of which is now on file and a matter of record in this office.

IN WITNESS WHEREOF, I have hereunto set my hand and affixed my official seal.

DONE IN OFFICE at Raleigh, this the 9th day of,   August   1971

Secretary of State

By
Deputy Secretary of State

Supplied by Brenda Denzler

Eric took the position that the state funding shouldn't be limited to Chapel Hill, because there were people with autism throughout the state, and they needed access to the resources a TEACCH Center could provide.

Through the TEACCH program, beginning in 1972, Eric was able to show that most autistic children did not suffer from mental disorders, as was believed by many at the time. He also demonstrated that parents of autistic children could be effective collaborators in the treatment and education of their children. Because the TEACCH program was now statewide, Eric's methods were rolled out in North Carolina schools and the special state-funded centers.

Gary Mesibov came to UNC for his postdoctoral work in 1973. Gary was assigned to work with Eric, and that was his introduction to autism. For several years he worked with Eric as his mentor under federal and state grants, and then in 1978, he was officially added to the TEACCH staff, became assistant director in 1988, and then, in 1993, became director when Eric retired from that position, although Eric remained active in a consultant role until his death in 2006.

At his retirement party, Eric called his recommendation that Gary replace him as director "the best decision I have ever made."

Eric had started the ball rolling toward changing perceptions and understandings about autism and particularly encouraging the treatment of parents as partners of professionals, not as clients of doctors. What Eric had begun, Gary built upon for his entire forty-four-year career, first with Eric, until his death in 2006, and then with the many staff members whom Gary had trained and worked with from the 1970s until he retired as a consultant in 2018.

Lee Marcus, clinical director at the Chapel Hill TEACCH Center for many years, Mary Beth Van Bourgondien, and Kathy Hearsey were among the pioneers who helped adapt, sustain, and improve TEACCH. Lee describes some of the early efforts of TEACCH to address the needs of people with ASD and their families:

> I knew I disagreed with some of the prevailing views at the time. I started in 1974 with the TEACCH Program, and I was occasionally working with DDDL, the Division of Developmental Disabilities and Learning. Gary was a psychologist doing postdoctoral work.

There were three TEACCH centers at the time, and I came to be director of the Chapel Hill Center. The numbers gradually went up to nine [centers], then down to six; then they added Raleigh. This was over a period of years.

In 1978 Gary was hired in the role of director of adolescent and adult services—I was already clinical director of the Chapel Hill TEACCH Center. Gary said he thought he understood everything about autism and TEACCH but found that making the correct diagnosis was very challenging.

Pre-1993 Gary and I developed models for people who were older. Gary and I would meet in the empty UNC football stadium to discuss our work. We each had family tickets to football games, but once the kids were out of the nest, we converted to individual tickets and would go to the games together. We'd meet for a scotch at Siena Hotel (we both liked scotch, although in moderation).

I always thought he was the best psychologist I ever knew. He had a way of getting to the heart of things and explaining and showing a depth of understanding. His writing was always clear. Any time I sent him an email, there was a prompt reply. He could manage his schedule so he was always available.

Anne McGuire, North Carolina, is a TEACCH autism specialist who is currently an educational coach for the Eastern Band of the Cherokee Indians Head Start program. Anne recalls,

I taught in Birmingham, Alabama, for twelve years beginning in 1978. In those days if identified children talked, they were classified as schizophrenic; if they didn't talk, they were labeled autistic. When I took the job in Birmingham, one of the other teachers was familiar with the TEACCH program, and so this had sparked an interest in me. Finally I visited the TEACCH Center in Asheville, and I was offered a job.

By the mid-1980s, Eric, the director, and Gary, his assistant, are an established team. How did TEACCH emerge from its small beginnings in 1972 with funding from the North Carolina state legislature into the 2020s as a worldwide resource across six continents in the field of autism?

As with anything that starts from scratch, there was a combination of fortuitous timing and having the expertise and readiness to take advantage of opportunities. You could say it all began to blossom in the native country of my favorite fictitious detective, Hercule Poirot. A man named Theo Peeters was the catalyst, and Kaia Mates, Kathy Hearsey, and Mary Beth Van Bourgondien described how Belgium became the catalyst for TEACCH connections throughout Europe. Each person was involved with TEACCH in a different way:

- Kathy transferred from Michigan in 1977 to UNC where she graduated with a BA in psychology and an M.Ed. in Special Education. She began her employment with TEACCH in Chapel Hill in 1987 and is currently director of TEACCH training.
- Mary Beth came to UNC as an intern in 1978 and has been a TEACCH faculty member and professor since 1981.
- Kaia is an autism specialist who has worked with TEACCH in various capacities from 1979 until she recently retired.

Gary conducted TEACCH training at the first international TEACCH conference held in Belgium, consisting of two separate one-week sessions.

Kaia Mates reflects on how TEACCH was introduced to Belgium by Theo Peeters, who was a journalist and a college professor:

After writing an article on autism for a weekly magazine, Peeters got interested in autism, and in 1982, he received a grant to do research on what was happening around the world.

By 1985 Peeters had been to North Carolina with his family and had studied with Gary. Two Raleigh classroom teachers had been working with Gary and me: Marian Wooten (now Troxler), an elementary teacher who taught a class for autistic children, and also Debbie Nay, a high school teacher who worked with children with autism. Theo suggested, "Let's do training for classroom teachers." The idea of putting kids with autism in the same classrooms with other students was unique even though we were trying out this kind of training on a small scale. In Chapel Hill we were working with only six or seven teachers at a time. In Belgium we were going to have twenty-five teachers. So we had to learn how to expand our model to train larger groups.

Kathy Hearsey added that in 1985, the team of Kaia, Marian, and Debbie, along with Gary and Theo, "conducted the first five-day hands-on training in a demonstration classroom. In fact this was the first time that this training was conducted anywhere. Then in 1986 the training was conducted for two weeks in Belgium and then four weeks in Chapel Hill for the first time in the United States.

Kaia continues the story:

> TEACCH had offered advice for teachers by sending trainers into the classroom—Eric started it in the '60s, but now we were still learning how to speak with diverse audiences and sizes of groups.
>
> We established that ASD children needed different approaches than kids with other disabilities, including Down syndrome and others. Then Peeters invited us to train in Belgium. The following year, 1986, we went to Belgium and trained ten to twenty teachers a week for two weeks. Gary was the one who conceptualized this training model. What Gary started in 1985 is the model used to train teachers throughout the world. There are three parts: (1) hands-on [work] with students in classrooms for at

least four hours, and this would include demonstrations with the students; (2) discussion; [and] (3) didactic learning lecture—new information.

Gary likes routines. If he thinks something is working, he sticks with it—he would accept new ideas but would stick with the basic principles that were making something work. When I started, training was very intense, almost one on one, because not that many teachers were involved.

When Theo said, "I have more than five teachers; I have forty for you to train," Gary expanded the model. This is where economics came in. We would need four or five hours in the classroom and a staff of four or five for the discussions if we were to replicate on a larger scale in Belgium what we were doing in Chapel Hill.

Steve Love, former clinical director with Asheville TEACCH Center (eighteen years) and licensed psychologist with Olson Huff Center for Child Development (ten years) recalled that Gary's comment upon departing for Belgium for the first time was, "If it's a flop, no one will know; if it's a success, we'll broadcast it across the United States."

The spread of TEACCH training throughout Europe—and ultimately the world—was fostered by two outcomes resulting from that initial trip to Belgium:

- People high up in autism research and practice in Sweden, Denmark, and other European countries started attending TEACCH training in Belgium in subsequent years and then inviting TEACCH to send teams to their countries.
- Belgian trainers who had been trained by TEACCH began accepting invitations to train in neighboring countries.

Like a slinky starting its journey down a staircase, the momentum of TEACCH around the world was becoming irreversible and inevitable.

Since European countries are much more centralized than the United States, when a few key people buy into something, it spreads rapidly.

Circumstances also brought TEACCH to Asian countries, and ultimately Russia, Saudi Arabia, and other faraway places. By 1980 Eric had already begun offering presentations in Japan where there was little available for families with a child with ASD, so when Japanese researchers learned of TEACCH and experienced results with it, they quickly embraced its principles.

Toshiyuki Fukuda of the Asahi Shimbun Social Welfare Organization explains:

> In January 1989 we had four wonderful trainers come to Japan in the persons of Dr. Schopler, Dr. Mesibov, Kathy Hearsey, and Kaia Mates. Can you imagine the surprise and excitement that was generated in all of the 40 participants in the seminars? To them everything was fresh . As a direct result, all the trainees became trainers, and with Dr. Sasaki as the core, seminars and study counseling are now constantly conducted throughout Japan.

Toshiyuki Fukuda, Gary, Kathy Hearsey, Kaia Mates

Tomoko Haramaki, a clinical psychologist, is president of the Japanese TEACCH Certified Professionals Network, is TEACCH certified, and runs a clinic in Saga, a town about a two hour flight from Tokyo, across the water from Korea. She works exclusively with people with autism. Tomoko has been to Chapel Hill for training many times and has invited and hosted Gary on many of his trips to Japan. In Tomoko's view, "Gary was an apostle, an evangelist. His preaching made the difference for us in Japan to know what autism is."

Kay Shigematsu, frequently Gary's interpreter and also a visitor to Chapel Hill for training, told me, "In Japan when I would be with him, he was a hero."

Discussing the growing impact of TEACCH in the United States, Kaia Mates says that

> Around this time (late 1980s), the ASA (Autism Society of America) had a grant to train teachers in Maine, Georgia, and Florida. Gary managed and developed that training in addition to developing services. The grant was about training teachers. In July he brought in teachers from throughout North Carolina. The grant allowed Gary to formulate a training program.

Signe Naftel, hired as a TEACCH trainer in 2002, says,

> People came from all over the country for our weeklong training during four weeks in July. Gary ran the training with a team of staff members. While each person comes for a week, the staff of TEACCH conducts the training for a different group for each of four weeks."

Anne McGuire explains,

> I had always wanted to learn about TEACCH. I had visited its center and took a job that was offered in 1989. Like most of the

trainers, I had the role of a generalist. I interviewed parents of children with autism coming to the center, consulted in classrooms, and administered PEPR diagnostic tests, which had been developed by Eric, his wife, and Gary. Suddenly I was given the position of clinical supervisor, and I was mentoring six new people coming in as therapists and editing their writing.

What attracted me to TEACCH? I definitely liked the philosophy of the program: parents and therapists are a team; parents are experts on their own children; therapists have their expertise in the scientific and therapeutic aspects of autism. I liked the structure. You look at behavioral problems as difficulties with communication, not as something good or bad.

Susan Moreno says,

The first time I heard the word TEACCH, it was my first conference, and talking with parents, all you heard about was TEACCH. In the 1980s North Carolina was way ahead of other states with services for people with autism and their families.

Mary Beth Van Bourgondien adds,

Another major contribution of Gary's to the TEACCH program [was] his development of services for adolescents and adults with autism and their families. He began with social skill groups; then he helped to advocate for the 1985 legislation that led to adding adult-focused therapists at the TEACCH centers; then he started the Supported Employment (SE) program; and then the Carolina Living and Learning Center (CLLC), a residential and vocational program for adults with profound autism. The CLLC provides active engagement and treatment for residents across a variety of skill areas: social, emotional, communication, leisure, vocational, and adaptive behaviors. Jemma Grindstaff, who describes herself as "a student of Gary's for 32 years since I was eighteen," has been CLLC director since January 2022.

Cory Shulman Head of the Autism Center, Hebrew University of Jerusalem, in Israel, comments,

The social groups that Gary created and that TEACCH promotes are so important. I shadowed Gary in Chapel Hill for about three weeks one summer; I believe it was in 1985. I remember his commitment to the participants and some really good ideas. Once we took a trip to the library and used the library system to teach the importance of keeping things organized and putting things back where they belong. I came from that meeting with the following mantra: "Everything has a place. Once you find it, keep it."

Chapter Five

TEACCH: A Tale of Two Cultures

> Gary's articulation of the culture of autism tied everything together and helped us understand autism.
>
> Lee Marcus

Part One: The Culture of Autism

If there was one observation that surfaced more than any other about Gary's contributions to TEACCH, it was his articulation of the culture of autism.

Cory Shulman says,

> It gave us a way of looking at people with ASD other than as people with a disability or as people with a lower intelligence, which is simply not true of them.

Mary Beth Van Bourgondien relates,

> One of Gary's greatest contributions to the field of autism was his way of being able to clearly articulate the learning style of

individuals with autism and the strength-based approach to working with individuals with autism developed at TEACCH. Long before the current neurodiversity approach, Gary talked about the culture of autism.

He recognized and shared the many strengths of individuals with autism and how by capitalizing on these visual strengths we could help autistic individuals build the skills they need to be successful. From the perspective of culture, he also articulated how some of the behaviors of children and adults with autism were just differences, not strengths or weaknesses, and needed to be respected.

Gary wrote that "Culture refers to shaped patterns of behavior." While recognizing that autism is not a culture according to a dictionary definition, he validates the comparison by stating that "Autism…affects the ways that individuals think, eat, dress, work, spend leisure time, and understand their world," all of which are elements of a culture. (Mesibov, Shea, and Schopler 2005)

Lee Marcus adds,

Gary's articulation of the culture of autism tied everything together and helped us understand autism. It is a handy tool to understand where a person of autism is coming from—how they view the world. Analogous is the culture of deafness. You need to think about this to be helpful—how difficult it is to pay attention and to process language. Culture is traditions, unique aspects, values, language of a particular society. Culture is the way a group of people see the world. This helps to explain autism to people in ways they can understand.

Thinking of autism as a culture is a way for professionals, trainers, and others to have respect for people with autism. When we think of autism as a culture, we don't think of people with autism as being weird. Imagine being dropped in a country where you know no one, don't speak the language, and don't understand the customs and traditions, and no one can read your emotions or you theirs. We need to see how they see the world—they are not weird; they just have a different perspective.

As Lee was asking us to think of how "we" would feel being dropped in a country where we know no one, I thought to myself, "What about a two-year-old who has no alternative ways to communicate except to cry, scream or throw a tantrum? How would a two-year-old react?"

Laura Klinger, who succeeded Gary as only the third director of TEACCH since Eric became sole director in 1976, brought to our attention that

> Most of us can learn particular social norms; we don't need things spelled out for us. Kids with autism need things spelled out. People with autism can't understand metaphors or figurative language.

Jayson Delisle, in his 25th year with the Supported Employment program, says,

> The first thing I learned when I came to Chapel Hill was Gary's writing about the culture of autism. They would hand this out to students. It made sense to me and began building the foundation of my understanding about autism and its place in our lives."

Kathy Hearsey speaks of her first visit to Belgium to conduct training when people from other European countries were also present and when she was training a group in which not all of the participants spoke English. It was a valuable experience for her and her colleagues because they had to communicate visually with the people who didn't speak English, and this was on-the-job training for what was necessary when trying to communicate with someone with ASD. But Kathy was a mature adult, and it was part of her job to accept the challenge of trying to communicate without words. People born with ASD only know that they are in a world where everyone else appears to understand each other, and they don't.

Maureen Bennie, a parent of two children with autism and founder/director of Autism Awareness Centre Inc., has a bachelor's degree in music and says,

> I trained [in music] in Germany and did not speak German. I was highly stressed for the first month before I began to calm down. The stress level was so high not being able to understand what everyone else seemed to grasp. Finally I was able to teach myself words and to use my knowledge of music to identify rhythms.

Catherine Davies, Indiana, TEACCH certified advanced consultant, says,

> I retrained as a clinical psychologist and was working in a National Health Service multidisciplinary team providing services for individuals with intellectual disabilities near London when I attended a three-day TEACCH training in 1997. That training was meaningful for me because the key element was to understand the culture of autism and from that bedrock build strategies, really taking [on] the perspective of the individual with autism and then using their strengths to support their weaknesses. Gary didn't present that specific training, but subsequently, I heard him talk many times about the cognition and learning styles of individuals with autism being key to the approach. He helped many people understand how and why you need to take a person-centered perspective; treat each person with autism as if they are unique and different from others labelled autistic.

I am moved by the response of Grayson Delisle, the twelve-year-old whom I asked to define autism. Grayson quite spontaneously told me,

> Autism is a different ability some people have that affects how people think. It's kind of cool because you are around people who think differently, so you would have more interesting conversations.

This is how we often view people from another country or people with totally different interests, habits, or viewpoints than ours: it's "cool." So, why can't we view people with autism as being "cool"?

None of us wants to be stereotyped by the standards applied to others. In school younger siblings resent the teacher who labels them because of experiences with an older sibling. Yet we tend to label all people with ASD based on our experience with one instead of recognizing that to meet one person with ASD is to meet one person with ASD. This is so unfair. It is even unfair to judge a person with ASD on the basis of his or her actions on a given day.

As David Moser, a man with autism told us,

> When you see me, I may seem fine. But see me after a tough day or in a morning when I am in a bad mood and am banging my head against a wall (literally)."

Svanhildur Kristjansson (Svany) is a speech-language pathologist and TEACCH trainer based in Arizona who frequently conducts training in Iceland, and she is the grandmother of four children diagnosed with autism. Svany explains that

> "Thinking of autism as a culture is respectful. The culture-of-autism concept, which was Gary Mesibov's idea, is always fitting into the

conversation when we talk about autism because it is respectful and accepting of differences—and fits the talk today about neurodiversity. I loved how he talked about the culture of autism. We need to accept all differences.

Cathy Pratt, director of Indiana Resource Center for Autism, Indiana Institute on Disability and Community, Indiana University since 2008, asserts that,

> The program was so strong because it started with the culture of autism. It starts with getting into the person's head and understanding how they think, and that informs everything they do. You must learn what are their strengths and weaknesses so you can use their strengths to help them overcome their weaknesses.
>
> I heard Gary speak many times of cognition and the need to know what's in their heads before thinking of strategies to address their behaviors. There is great strength in having real kids we can watch and learn about rather than impose on them what we want them to do.

Cory Shulman speaks again about the significance of the culture of autism, saying,

> One of the most important things I learned from my TEACCH training in Chapel Hill is that you need to think of autism as a culture, not as something to be fixed. It is a culture of its own. We have an obligation to accommodate people in the culture of autism just as we do easily when we are with people in any other culture.

Peter Vermeulen and Bernadette Dekeukeleire are married and continue to work with Belgian parental societies to provide information and services to families with autistic children. They told me of a dinner at the Kings Arms in Kent, England, where Peter talked about neurodiversity as a culture and why we should accept and cherish brains that are different. Peter quotes Gary as citing the *Cheers* bar in Boston as being a place where neurodiversity is celebrated. Peter remembers Gary saying,

> "Every character in the series has something that would probably be diagnosed nowadays, but in Cheers, everyone is welcome as who they are, even if they are not perfect." I still share Gary's idea about *Cheers* in my trainings, paying tribute to Gary. A little bit more *Cheers* would make the world a better place for autism."

Christine Edwards-Daem, chief executive at Kent Autistic Trust, invited Peter (right) and Gary for a one-day training on autism and happiness on July 1, 2016.

Joanne Quinn, certified TEACCH trainer in Rhode Island, executive director of The Autism Project, and parent of a child with ASD, says, "When I began thinking of people with ASD as people with different habits, strengths, and weaknesses than me rather than as people with a disability, it changed my entire view of them."

Part Two: The Culture of TEACCH

The number of staff members who have remained with the organization for many years is a significant strength of TEACCH. In the 2020s there have been frequent news reports indicating that a record number of employees are changing jobs. Yet Kathy Hearsey and Mary Beth Van Bourgondien were with Gary almost from the beginning, as was Lee Marcus prior to his retirement in 2008, and so many more staff members are or were with TEACCH for between ten and twenty-five years. When an organization retains this many employees for many years, it speaks to the culture of the organization.

Steve Kroupa and Kyoko Tanaka met during TEACCH training in Chapel Hill in 2005, were reunited when Steve was in Japan to conduct training in 2007, were married in 2011, and have lived in Japan and continued working with people with autism since then. Kyoko is a child psychiatrist and has a brother with autism. Steve says,

> TEACCH is one of only two organizations I have worked for in my lifetime that created its own culture of excellence. Gary understood this, and it is something that Japanese people readily recognize, as this concept is well known in Japanese culture and pursued by the best companies like Sony and Toyota. Gary created a culture of TEACCH that made it fun and productive to work there. This culture involved:
>
> - a consensus view of the world
> - the integrity of leadership
> - hiring staff with strong professional credentials and personal qualities and values that matched the mission of the program
> - being really good at respecting and empowering others

Joanie Berry was employed twenty-five years by TEACCH beginning in 1985, and she was secretary to Gary from 1995 to 2010. Joanie told me,

Gary and Eric made us feel that any contribution, however small, was important. I appreciated the family environment and the camaraderie. I did filing, typing reports, answering the phone, and welcoming visitors. I also helped them prepare for international visits, and they made me feel I was important. Gary particularly created this atmosphere. It was hard to out "thank" him. It became a game with us to try. Whatever you did, Gary would thank you for doing it and then thank you again for reporting to him what you had done. This kind of treatment of employees leads to a positive culture in an organization.

I can imagine how stressed Gary must have been at times, yet I don't recall any time he didn't come into the office with a smile and warm greeting and a "How'd you like that game last night?"

Gary always remained loyal to Stanford, but he was a keen follower of North Carolina basketball, as am I. One anecdote stays with me:

When storied coach Dean Smith retired in 1997 with 879 victories over the course of thirty-six years at UNC, there was going to be a 3:00 p.m. press conference. He was the only UNC coach I had known, and I was in tears most of the morning. Finally Gary called me into his office and said, "I want you to go home and watch the press conference from there, and I am going to go home and also watch the press conference and probably cry too. So at 3:00 pm, I watched the press conference and cried, and I imagine Gary did too.

Eric was awarded the American Psychological Association's Lifetime Achievement Award for his work developing TEACCH into a program of excellence, and he recognized that there is a special culture within the TEACCH program. In an article for the association's journal, Eric chose to highlight the essential qualities of TEACCH that he believed were instrumental in its effectiveness and success. He wrote that

The technical term for these qualities is "nonspecific treatment effect," and they pertain to the culture of the program, the characteristics and shared mission of the staff, the principles and values of the program, and, most importantly, the quality of relationships that the staff develop with clients, families, and the broader community. (Schopler, E. (1987). Specific and nonspecific factors in the effectiveness of a treatment system. *American Psychologist, 42*(4), 376–383.)

Gary Is Inspired to Focus on the Core Values of TEACCH

Many of the people with whom I spoke credit Gary for the decision to establish a set of articulated core values for the TEACCH program. The idea resulted from a keynote speaker at UNC, Dr. Robert Allen, who impressed Gary when he referred to a Stanford University Business School study that attempted to identify what excellent and visionary companies had in common. According to Gary in the book he cowrote with Victoria Shea and Eric (*The TEACCH Approach to Autism Spectrum Disorders*, 2005), the common elements were not exceptional leadership, strategic planning mission statements, or profit margins. Instead it was a core ideology, "a sense of values and purpose beyond just making money that were clearly articulated and understood throughout the company. These core values varied from company to company."

Gary believed that TEACCH fit the pattern of progressive organizations, so in the early 2000s, he sent out a questionnaire to ask his staff what they saw as the core values of TEACCH. After Gary and the leadership of TEACCH reviewed the survey results, the core values were reduced to writing and are generally referred to as the "principles of TEACCH":

- We understand and appreciate that people with autism spectrum disorder are our highest priority.

- We are committed to excellence and have a strong work ethic.
- TEACCH professionals don't stand on ceremony or become overly impressed with their status, discipline, or position.
- A spirit of cooperation and collaboration characterizes all of our work.
- We look for the best in others and in ourselves.

In 2020, TEACCH added a new core value and updated the originals, as described in its 2020 annual report, "to demonstrate our commitment to diversity, equity, and inclusion."

Principles of TEACCH

Often as I spoke with certified TEACCH trainers, they would refer to the principles of TEACCH, which, as David Preece, social worker, senior lecturer in Special Educational Needs and Inclusion at the University of Northampton, England explained that "The TEACCH principles have long been a given in the UK and many other countries."

According to David the principles of TEACCH include:

- Conducting an ongoing assessment of needs to develop individualized interventions
- Developing independence through meaningful teaching and learning
- Building on strengths and interests of students with autism.
- Making use of visual strengths by providing individualized visual structure
- Involving parents as coeducators

Current TEACCH director Laura Klinger sent me this official TEACCH Philosophy:

TEACCH Philosophy

- Unique Learning Styles

- Family Collaboration

- Whole Person View

- Structured TEACCHing

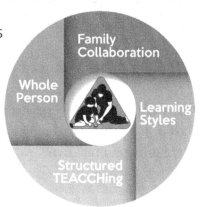

Graphic supplied by Laura Klinger

As is evident, the principles cited by David Preece are consistent with, and an elaboration of, the philosophy officially ascribed to TEACCH in the preceding graphic.

Steve Kroupa says,

> Gary's TEACCH director meetings were always fun, and this was partly because Gary was always calm, offered interesting insights, and had a sense of humor and valued what the other directors had to say. His humor was subtle, clever, and humble.

Kaia Mates adds,

> Gary created a family of those of us who worked with him. Certain interns were very important to him."

Signe Naftel also "loved working at TEACCH with Gary."

Marie Howley, England, autism specialist teacher and university of Northampton senior lecturer, sums it all up:

> At TEACCH we are all like a family. Just hearing the names of my former colleagues from TEACCH gives me a warm feeling. Gary gave us that. He was so good at making you feel you belonged.

Chapter Six

Stories from Five Parents of Children with Autism

If you've met one person with autism, you've met
one person with autism.

Stephen Shore

Eric had focused the world on treating parents as partners, and Gary continued the development of strategies for relying on parents as the experts on their children.

David Preece says of Gary,

He really cultivated an openness and humility in professionals. This, I think, is one of the things I really learned from Gary—a humility and willingness to listen to parents. Not to come in as the expert with all the answers and, if something is not working, to say, "Well, you're just doing it wrong." But to say, "I may be the expert in autism, but you're the expert regarding your child, so let's put our heads together to try and work this out."

This chapter has narrations by five parents of children with autism, each child presenting different behaviors and each with different challenges for their parents. Maureen Bennie and her husband have two children with autism, two years apart in age, and Maureen says that their experiences with the first child provided no guidance for supporting the younger.

Why are people with autism so different from each other? With a quick Internet search, I came up with a list of twenty-one possible behaviors that can indicate someone has ASD. Many experts cite these eight:

- Avoidance of eye contact or poor eye contact[1]
- Behavioral problems
- Deficits in language comprehension
- Inappropriate social interaction
- Intense focus on one topic
- Lack of empathy
- Not engaging in play with peers*
- Preoccupation with specific topics*

Of course, it must be remembered that people classified as having ASD are as different from each other as a bird is from a fish. A person with ASD may exhibit any one or two of these behaviors while not exhibiting any of the others.

Kyoko Tanaka created a list of the kinds of strengths and challenges that people with autism may display:

- Types of strengths: visual learning, numbers, bluntness
- Types of challenges: auditory language, literal interpretations, bluntness

Susan Moreno

Susan Moreno, founder of MAAP Services for Autism, was mentored by Gary when she was growing her organization. Like many people who are

---

[1] Early symptoms and signs in babies.

now trainers or resource providers for families with ASD children, Susan did not grow up expecting to work in the field of autism. Advances in research and understanding of autism are due largely to the efforts of parents like Susan. Many, finding a scarcity of information to guide them with their own autistic child, developed the support services that now exist, and many have participated in parent support groups that contributed to lobbying efforts for governmental funding. Here is Susan's story:

Our daughter Beth was born in March 1972. Almost immediately, and continuing as she developed, we began to think that we, as new parents, were doing something wrong:

- Beth would only sleep two hours per night.
- She would have terrible sleep disturbances.
- She never looked at us.
- She walked on her toes all the time.
- She wouldn't socialize with other children.
- She had meltdowns that could last up to twelve hours.

When Beth was turning two, I went to a *Mommy and Me* workshop on how to care for children. A respected psychologist asked us, "Have you noticed she is the only one of eighteen children not playing with the others, and she is the second oldest of the eighteen?"

This psychologist asked me: "What do you enjoy doing?" I said I enjoy spending time with Beth. She said, "But what are the personal things you do?"

I said, "I play guitar for Beth."

"No, no," she said, "What do you do that doesn't involve Beth?"

This awakened me to the importance of taking four or five hours a week for myself, and so I employed a woman who would take care of Beth for a few hours a week. After having Beth a few times, she pointed out to me that Beth could get hysterical for no apparent reason. That's when I made an appointment with the diagnostic clinic at UCLA's Neuropsychiatric Institute. I had to wait three months to get in. While waiting for the date of my appointment, I saw a documentary on TV about autism. It presented the most severe cases and ended with a parent who had killed his autistic child, saying the equivalent of, "He was in such [a] bad condition, he is better off now."

Thinking these were people with much worse situations than ours, we were temporarily relieved—Beth couldn't be autistic.

But then Beth, two and a half, went through a month of diagnostic tests. Imagine what we thought when an intern and a three-doctor team gave us the diagnosis that Beth was autistic, having just seen that documentary. We were fortunate because the three doctors on the team, it turned out, were to become leaders in their field. These were still the times when the belief was that "refrigerator mothers" caused autism in their children. They assured us that this was not due to our parenting. Less qualified doctors might not have correctly diagnosed Beth's situation, and it was this diagnosis that at least started us up the right path toward giving Beth a fulfilling quality of life.

I began seeking resources and started by contacting the National Society for Autistic Children (NSA).

In 1984 I started a newsletter for parents. At a conference in Omaha, Nebraska, there was an ad for parents of high-functioning people with autism to come to a meeting. Twenty-five people showed up, and that's when I realized the extent of autism in its higher-functioning form. We agreed it would be good to have a way of sharing our situations and ideas. So I took contact information from everyone.

A year later I hadn't heard from anyone of the other twenty-four, and none of them had contacted another, so I wrote a letter, photocopied it, and mailed it to each of the twenty-four individuals, asking if they would share the name, age, gender, and interests of their autistic child. Twenty-three wrote back. Over the years our newsletter grew to an audience of thousands in 119 countries. Eventually we were able to turn them into emails. We ended newsletters with "You are not alone." Because of Gary and what he started, this is no longer needed—the services and information are readily available.

My daughter is now fifty. The experts had told me that she might never recognize us as her parents. The only response she ever gave the doctors at UCLA who were diagnosing her was to say, "Kitty meow." We left that initial diagnosis meeting at UCLA thinking we might have her taken away from us to be institutionalized, which we would never have allowed.

By the time she graduated from high school, Beth had been fully included in classes. She did poorly on the SATs, but the questions were timed, and she was not afforded any accommodations. She is currently an expert on Gregorian chants, has a master's in church music and liturgy, [and] sings professionally as a church cantor and at weddings and funerals. She rents a house from us where she does her own cooking and laundry. She also speaks three languages.

Beth's success and achievements were greatly enhanced by Gary's wonderful mentoring and encouragement.

Joanne Quinn
Joanne Quinn is Executive Director of Rhode Island's "The Autism Project."

My son Patrick was diagnosed when he was four. He never had tantrums; he would just find ways to run away from us. His teachers and the first few doctors we took him to thought he was ADD.

Finally we took him to a hospital for a diagnosis, and after eight hours, they told us he was provisional high-level autistic.

Two strategies immediately brought a change in Patrick's behavior, so if nothing else, a parent should use countdown times and "first this and then." The "first" might be to "finish homework," and the "then" would be the treat, which could be food or a chance to play something he likes. If nothing else it instantly takes the chaos out of your life.

Training for parents must start with: What is autism, and why are interventions important?

If I asked Patrick questions, he didn't throw tantrums, but he would walk away from me. I had to write things down: "What are three things you did in school today?"

Like many who [have] ASD, Patrick is not auditory. He would ask me, "Mom, can you write more of those stories?"

I would write "What is Halloween?" "What is…?"

Patrick is now mayor of East Greenwich, Rhode Island. He still works by calendars, but now he has control over his life. He still needs lots of support, but he has his own apartment. He even figured out how to turn on the CC on the TV so that he could read the captions if he had difficulty understanding the audio.

Alice Wertheimer

In 1984 Alice's daughter Rachel was born; in 1986 her son David was born. Alice and Pierre Wertheimer lived in New Jersey when David, two years old, was diagnosed as autistic.. According to Alice,

The proximity of our children's ages helped us to notice that they were proceeding differently. People assured us it was normal for girls and boys to develop at different rates.

In 1988 my father suddenly died, and I thought David's behavior, which was regressing, was his reaction to my grief. He had been doing things all toddlers do and then suddenly stopped about the time my father died. He had been seeing my father almost daily, so I concluded his regression was due to this event.

However, when David was two and a half, I became alarmed. David had become difficult and very much out of control. He was very unhappy, couldn't communicate; he was reducing his diet, wouldn't eat, screamed all day and night, and it was very discouraging. His lack of eating really scared me as a mother.

We took David to one doctor after another. Finally someone said it was autism. What we were experiencing with David was not at all what I pictured of autism. I was naïve about it. While attitudes were gradually changing, it was not very long before that when mothers were held responsible and blamed for a child's autism.

I went to the library and found all the books by Eric and Gary that they cowrote in the 1980s. Then I was put in touch with this group of mothers of autistic children in New Jersey, where I was. I wasn't going to join their group, but one of the mothers called me, and she was so upbeat and laughing. And she helped me realize that my son's perspective was unique, and he could be so funny.

I agreed to meet with her and her group, and it was wonderful. We met by the shore. Some parents told me of this tutor who came to their homes once or twice a week and that this tutor had been trained in Chapel Hill at this TEACCH program. We hired her to work with David as often as she could, which turned out to be twice a week. She connected with David immediately. Within a month we saw differences in his behavior. The tutor was a full-time schoolteacher working with autistic children, and she did tutoring on her own. She was originally from Tennessee but was living and working in New Jersey.

The evidence of how quickly she bonded with David was that

as soon as he would hear her knocking at the door, he would pick up his little toddler's chair, take it to the table where they would work, and wait for her to join him.

The tutor was firm with David, whereas I was often reluctant to provide him with the structure he required. The tutor worked on language development. She focused on the visual. "It is most important," she told us, "not to bombard him with language." Use visuals—signs like a stop sign instead of telling him to stop doing something. Redirect him to positive things. For instance, if he has free time when you fear he might do something unacceptable, move him toward a game he likes or encourage him to do something by himself that you know he likes to do.

The tutor told us that while the amount of chaos in the house was OK and typical for most children, it was overstimulating for a child with autism. For example, tons of toys and videos covered the floor as the tutor entered our home, and she immediately said, "This is too much stimulation. We'll set up a timer for your toddler, and then when the time is up, we'll move on to just one other activity, and we'll focus on one thing at a time." We had been doing what most parents do: leaving out on the floor all kinds of toys, some that make noise and some a child can move around.

Actually, I'm now using the same strategies with a childhood friend who has early onset Alzheimer's. People with Alzheimer's, like those with ASD, have difficulty with verbal language.

In 1989 [after I had] read some of their writings, although not having met them, Eric and Gary became like gods to me. Because David's tutor had been trained at TEACCH in Chapel Hill, I called a friend who was a neighbor of Gary's, and she said, "You should talk with Gary Mesibov."

I said, "Oh, no, he's not going to talk with me."

My friend said, "Call him at home."

I did, and he was so nice. He said, "I think you should talk with

Lee Marcus if you are considering moving here." He said he would contact Lee, and Lee would be in touch with me. Lee called the next day, and while Lee retired in 2008, he still talks with David monthly.

Little had I known at the time, but throughout the world, parents who had a child with autism were calling Gary, and he was getting calls like mine every day.

The people at TEACCH, led by TEACCH Center director Lee Marcus in particular, were so generous with their time. Lee and a colleague were running a unique preschool as part of the TEACCH services. Both Lee and Gary stressed the need to get David down here for the start of the preschool year. So we moved immediately to Chapel Hill! Preschool was wonderful. It put us on a learning curve for one whole year. David still works at TEACCH. He is still coached by someone assigned to him as part of the Supported Employment program that Gary started.

The process of having David diagnosed in New Jersey, starting at age two, was stressful and frightening. When we had visited neurologists, psychologists, speech therapists, and went from doctor to doctor before discovering TEACCH, each focused on his weaknesses and told us what he couldn't do, which we already knew. That's why we were taking him to doctors. We got a lot of information that was negative, and it seemed like everyone we visited was telling us negative things we already knew:

- He can't eat
- He has difficulty with words
- He wakes up crying
- He is easily frustrated
- He does not connect with other children
- He does not play with toys appropriately
- He does not even connect to the people assessing him

However, when we walked into the TEACCH building and met the professionals, the reactions to David were totally different. We took the elevator up, and when the door opened, David rushed out and raced down the hallway. Unlike every other place we had been to, Lee Marcus and the members of his team smiled, and Lee said, "Oh, he's so cute." David was cute, but that's not how other experts had seen him. To Lee and his team, David, with his curly blond hair and enthusiastic race down the hall, was just like any other four-year-old boy. This was the start of our experience with TEACCH people; they focused on the many things David could do, not what he couldn't.

The entire approach of TEACCH is to focus on strengths and to use them to overcome weaknesses. Until we found TEACCH, I was a very challenged mother with a very challenged child. I thought I must be a poor parent. I was so down on myself, and I was down on David, and there they were, recognizing how cute this four-year-old boy is.

TEACCH recognized how important parental support was to the progress of the child with autism. Hence TEACCH started:

- mothers' groups
- fathers' groups
- siblings' groups
- social groups

They started monthly outings—camping and other activities. They taught us how to talk to our child and how to talk to others about our child. They modeled it. The supports were built into the system.

Gary had a huge impact on our lives, as did TEACCH. Gary would say David had good material inside him. Without what we got from TEACCH, he would not be living on his own as he is now. When David might not get invited to a party, he could have a party with other autistic kids in his TEACCH organized group.

David is now living on his own. He has a place in Chapel Hill. He is conversant and can definitely let you know his needs. He used to be very rigid. In fact, Lee used to refer to him as David "Rigid" Wertheimer. If he did something one way, it always had to be that way. Now he comes to our house on weekends and is willing to compromise: "Oh, Mom, I can do it that way if you want."

His appetite, which used to be very limited, is now much wider than many people his age. He cooks his own food and likes to try recipes. He may need guidance at times, but he likes to try new things. This came about gradually by learning to communicate and wanting to observe others. David is now a very happy and productive citizen who lives independently.

All of his progress has been gradual but inexorable.

Alice Wertheimer with Gary at a 2013 TEACCH Roast Award event for Gary

Maureen Bennie

Maureen Bennie is founder and director of Autism Awareness Centre, Calgary, Canada (established 2003). Her son, Mark, "is twenty-five and was diagnosed with ASD when he was two years and ten months old on December 3, 1999." Her daughter, "Julia, is twenty-three years old and was officially diagnosed with ASD a year and several months after she was born." Maureen is another parent with no previous knowledge of autism who then became an expert in the field out of necessity. Maureen explains,

> There were no family-member support services at that time (1999). In fact, when I walked out of the hospital with Mark's diagnosis, they handed me five pamphlets, and that was it. I had to do it all. I started doing my own research in 2003, when I realized we were not going to find outside help. And there wasn't much on the internet at that time, certainly not about autism. Finding information about autism was like searching for the proverbial needle in a haystack.
>
> My website now has a library of over nine hundred titles. I blog twice a month; the last one was on resilience, and the next will be on how long it takes children with ASD to acquire skills. I train trainers who then go out to different parts of Canada and other countries to conduct training. I do this to help others.
>
> While to others it might seem that a parent's second child with autism would be easier, Maureen points out that the behaviors and challenges of her two children were completely different:
>
> It was very hard to cope with it the second time. It was three years before I could go back to work as a high-school music teacher, and I finally went back because I wanted to end my teaching career on a high note.
>
> I had a Bachelor of Music degree and a minor in English. I was specializing in classical music. My doctor suggested that I give up Julia for adoption. I wouldn't think of it, and Ron, my husband, said,

"We'll die before we put our daughter up for adoption." I took three years off from teaching while I recovered emotionally and started to learn what we had to do to support our child and then children.

It was doubly difficult because each child was so different that what we did with Mark didn't transfer to Julia. Our son wouldn't go to bed until 10:00 p.m. and our daughter would awaken at midnight. I can actually sleep standing up with my back against a wall because I had to learn to do that while functioning on just a few hours' sleep raising two children with ASD while they were toddlers.

We enrolled Mark in the New Heights Early Learning Service School, and we started to get connected to staff there. New Heights was using TEACCH philosophy, and we adopted what they were doing in their school to our work with our own children and then our work at conferences and training trainers.

Gary has been one of the great innovators in structure and building scaffolding. TEACCH emphasizes visual and kinesthetic learning and learning to break tasks into steps, one at a time. When people with autism get stuck at a step, it increases their frustration, and therefore it is critical to have steps built in so you can lead them a step at a time and also show them what the last step will be. People with autism need predictability. How does a person with autism know when a task is over? It can be very stressful not knowing. People with autism need to know what the last step in a task will be, or they get anxious.

Scaffolding examples include putting in supports around people such as routines, a schedule, visual cues. TEACCH has given us structure through visuals. For instance, here is how you can let them know when a task will be over: They could be picking things off a piece of paper, and you let them know the task is over when there is nothing left on the paper. Or you can set a timer, and then the person can see as it runs down toward the end of the task. There must be a visual. Many children, particularly those under four years of age, won't know what you mean when you say, "ten minutes."

Before you can teach someone skills, they need to have prerequisite skills. For instance, to learn the alphabet, you need to know categories—can they sort by colors?—and TEACCH gave us the methods to break this into steps. People with ASD are often weak on auditory skills, which is why the emphasis must be on visual and kinesthetic teaching and learning.

Lori Ireland

Lori Ireland is one of the founders of Extraordinary Ventures (EV). Formed in 2007, EV is a sustainable business model and is one unique solution addressing the employment dilemma adults with autism often face. EV competes in the marketplace and provides employment opportunities for people with ASD. This is Lori's story:

In 1994 we moved from LA to Chapel Hill because there were no good services in LA, and we didn't want a behavioral focus, which was all that was offered there that we could locate. Our four-year-old son, diagnosed with autism, had been in a partial hospitalization program at UCLA. While there was no longer electric shock treatment, there were still some programs, not the one our son was in, where parents were required to sign a paper acknowledging [the service provider's] right to hit their child.

TEACCH brought us together with other families at a time when autism was not widely known. There were family groups; kids could get together, and there was a mom's group. Our son went to a demonstration school that was run by TEACCH. Alice Wertheimer and others were already working with the local schools, and because of others who preceded me, I eventually became chairperson of the Autism Society of America. My husband was chair of the Autism Science Foundation.

As parents we came to realize that when a child with autism got out of the public school system, there were no more entitlements. School is the only entitlement. Eighty percent of people with autism are unemployed or underemployed. We decided to run a for-profit business, about 90 percent self-funded. People come and interview for a job. Ours is not a training program; we compete in the regular marketplaces.

Our son does pickup and delivery of laundry, and his job coach drives. If our son had nothing to do, it would be terrible. We are focused on supporting people and helping them make connections to live the kind of life they want to live—to have a quality of life. Connections include community, family, health-care resources, educational support, and counselling.

At one time we were in a quandary about letting our son spend time living in a different house. Gary offered sound advice: "Just because he has one routine now doesn't mean he couldn't have two." Our son is now in a very predictable low-stimulation setting and living nearby. After an initial adjustment, he is comfortable in his new setting, and he visits us at our home on a regular basis.

The Autism Society of North Carolina was formed in 1970 by a group of parents who wanted to build better lives for their children with autism. The parents—including JoAnn Jeffries, Betty Camp, and Mary Lou "Bobo" Warren—did not accept that their children were unreachable or should be excluded from school or community life.

The parents created the organization to share information, provide support to one another, and improve the lives of children with autism in the state. The founders laid the groundwork for the services and supports these families and individuals now enjoy. Their goals remain part of our mission today.

Chapter Seven

Stories from Two Adults with Autism

I'm OK; it's the rest of the world that has a problem.
Matthew Hardie, a man with autism

This chapter includes narrations by two men with ASD, one of whom, David, describes his "quirks" and his experiences getting diagnosed, going through schooling, and now with gainful employment. The other, Matthew, also with gainful employment, speaks of why he resorted to throwing things when he was growing up. Both discuss the bullying they endured.

David Moser

David Moser is a person with high-functioning ASD. He grew up outside of Asheville, North Carolina, went to Asheville High School and college at the University of Northern Colorado, and attended graduate school at Appalachian University.

David had been an accounting technician at the TEACCH Center in Chapel Hill for twenty-seven and a half years when we spoke in February

2022. He works in an administrative capacity on the same floor where Eric and Gary had offices when David began his career working for TEACCH.

Here is David's story:

I was diagnosed as [having] hyperactive ADHD in school but not as autistic. Like a lot of people with higher-level Asperger's, I can be either easily distracted or highly focused. I didn't start talking until age four. We were at Cape Canaveral, and a stranger asked me my name. I said, "My name is David Moser," and then I kept talking, and I would tell people I had four years to make up for.

When I wasn't speaking the first four years of my life, I got by a lot by gesturing. My cousins and my brother could be pretty chatty, so I was the man of few words, but I always knew how to get what I wanted. In third grade, I was at a sixth-grade reading level; in sixth grade, ninth-grade reading level; in ninth grade, college reading level. I love to read, and I love movies about complex themes or real-life situations. I'm not much for Marvel-type movies. It took me many years to get to this point. My autism bedeviled me in high school.

As a child I had a few "almost" diagnoses, and I did go to ADHD and dyslexia prep schools, where I learned to write. Sometimes I am dyslexic. I may confuse left and right or six and nine. However, I am practically ambidextrous—I can write almost as well, putt, or hit a baseball with either hand.

In school I was frequently bullied, so I would sit near the front of the room to be closer to the teacher. The bullying was because I was not well coordinated. I also feared a baseball coming at me at thirty-two feet per second. I got hit by a softball once and by a baseball, and they left their marks.

In high school and at UNC, I had tutoring, which helped. I would start projects early because if I left them for the last minute, it would be a mess. I have a need for structure; I can be very disorganized. I was a political science major, and I love politics. Vouchers got me into conservative Christian schools.

Some of my little quirks and foibles:

- For all my perfectionist tendencies, I can be personally disorganized.
- I can go through the day on a stream of consciousness, perhaps getting lost in my exhaustive music collection and without regard for appointments or commitments.
- I need my day planner and my Microsoft Outlook calendar. This is my brain helping me keep up with my appointments.
- Post-its are the greatest invention. I live my life by Post-it notes. I can take out my wallet in a store or pharmacy, and I can refer to my Post-it notes.

I was constantly amazed that Gary always had time for me; he would ask me about what I was doing and would take a real interest, not just asking because it was part of his job. He was the real thing, and he was a real friend to my parents. They called him at work after my car accident and when my boiler broke down, and I was highly agitated. He would talk me through it. He put people in my life like Kathy Hearsey, Jayson Delisle, and Mike Chapman. Not only could he help me personally when I needed him but he could put me in touch with the right people.

Gary initiated social-skills groups and got us all together. I had thought I was the only one on the spectrum. Then I found out there are others like me. Gary helped me find my best friends through these social groups, and he taught me how to make friends. I enjoyed it when Gary would take us to fine restaurants, but also lesser restaurants where we would go to just eat and talk. I loved going to Durham Bulls games and also went to Duke basketball games twice with Gary's son Todd.

What I like about Gary is he is always so accepting. He started the social groups [see chapter nine], and along with Kathy and Mary Beth, we would meet regularly.

I graduated UNC with a degree and then went to Appalachian University for my graduate degree but had a personality conflict with the head of the department, and he was the person leading my thesis committee. And there weren't as many supports for me as I had at UNC. They wouldn't let me switch classes when I made the request. I took real-estate courses and got a real-estate license, but this was not what I wanted.

My troubles with my thesis supervisor made things really tough. My autistic behaviors really came out. I got As in the classes I liked. Classes I couldn't stand I didn't finish. For the first time in my scholastic career, I got incompletes. At this time I was a mess and was faced with the possibility of flunking out. I can be a perfectionist, which is why I was a really good graduate assistant.

My parents saw a Barbara Walters special on autism with Temple Grandin. This included an autism checklist, and my parents said, "This is David." I met Temple Grandin when I was with Gary at a TEACCH conference around 2002. After the Walters show, my parents had me tested. I was told, "It's a good thing you are in North Carolina because TEACCH can help you with accommodations and might even be able to help you with grad school." I was diagnosed with ASD at the TEACCH Center by a great therapist, Dr. Steve Love.

I was still trying to finish college. I had a hearing related to my disability at Appalachian College, and I was absolved academically. It was decided that I could get a different thesis committee. I was twenty-five at the time, and a job opened up at TEACCH. Gary and Mike Chapman may have had something to do with this. They believed I could use my skills in the accounting department since I am obsessed with quality and good with numbers.

They believed I could learn some work skills, which I did.

So I chose to accept this position rather than continue in graduate school. I started working thirty hours a week, moved up to thirty-five after five years, and now for the past twenty years, I have worked forty hours a week. I got auditory training, too, along the way.

I do presentations, and I enjoy them. And I may continue doing them after retirement.

No two presentations are alike. It depends on the audience, the questions they ask, and the time allotted. I include in my presentations what I was like growing up, not speaking until I was four, and how effective use of visuals enables me to communicate with others and them to communicate with me. I don't know what my life would have been like if my folks hadn't seen the Barbara Walters show. And I owe a lot to Gary.

I did receive accommodations, including extra time on tests. My classmates liked having me around because it also gave them extra time. Also, I had special tutoring—more visual learning; more hands-on.

Why Should David Get Accommodations?

What do I say to people who say, "Well, it's OK to give him accommodations, but why should he get the same grade as others if he gets the accommodations, and they don't?" Some of my peers would ask this. Well, it takes me about twenty minutes to think something through that you might be able to do in a minute off the top of your head.

As an adjunct college professor I would sometimes be asked by a student in my class why someone who gets an accommodation should get the same grade as someone who achieves the same level of quality without an accommodation. "After all," some students would protest, "in the real world, you have to meet the requirements of your job, don't you?"

I thought about this and realized that in the real world, we all make our own accommodations as we need them, and nobody even knows what accommodations we may have made. In the real world, we are judged by results. I can take a day to prepare a report that a colleague might complete in two hours. Does anyone even know how long it took each of us? Does anyone care as long as we produce quality work? It is only in schools that we are confronted with someone telling us how long we have to complete a task when there doesn't need to be a deadline.

David concluded his story, saying,

> "Gary and I would often say, "The sun never sets on the TEACCH empire."

The sun never sets on TEACCH and that is evidence of what Eric and Gary have contributed to the field of autism and to the quality of life of David and so many other people with ASD, and their families.

Matthew Hardie

Matthew Hardie and his family live in England. Matt's mother, Annette, recalls,

> At his one-year birthday party (1988), it was clear that Matt was not engaged with the goings on. As he grew older, he was very active, although not interacting with others. He would climb on door frames and jump. You never knew when he would jump on you.
>
> When Matt was in nursery school, I was approached by a teacher who told me he needed more support. I noticed that all the

other young children in his class had a tin with words, but Matt did not have a tin. When I asked the teacher why, she said that "Matt doesn't need a tin of words because he'll never be able to read." So I got my own tin and used it the way his brother, older by three years, had also used the tin of words when he had been in the same nursery school.

At age four, Matt had no vocabulary; by age seven he was the best reader in the school. But his behavior was still off the wall.

In the early 1990s, no local schools had any idea how to deal with autism. Psychologists often gave us wrong information. One suggested we move furniture around, which was precisely the wrong thing to do for someone with ASD.

We are so thankful that the school psychologist put us in touch with Terry and Eileen Arnold. Without their guidance our lives would be drastically different. They explained things to us in ways we could understand. With their support, Ian [Matthew's father] and I became our own resource providers as well as setting up a support system for others.

I got speech therapy into the schools. I set up a parent support group which eventually achieved a database of over five hundred members and brought in guest speakers to our once-a-month meetings. Some of us would meet Mondays with David Preece and others. We pleaded with the local council for funding.

Matt picks up his story at this point:

As a child I realized I was different, but I was not sure why that was. I had my own agenda. I had no desire to socialize; I just wanted to play with my *Thomas the Tank Engine* toys or watch cartoons, and I preferred to be by myself. I would lose my temper if there was any change in my routine.

I did not always enjoy the sessions I had to attend with an additional-needs teacher in secondary school. I would be provided sheets of different cartoon faces (similar to emojis); actual photos of actual people would have been better in helping me identify facial expressions.

As I grew older, my behavior improved, and I lost many of my autistic traits. Apparently I would throw things at people, hitting children. I would say no to anything and everything.

There was a legendary puppet show I would watch on TV after school called *Sooty*. I rarely talked, and I would imitate one of the characters named Sweep using a squeaky voice. I just didn't want to use my voice.

In secondary school I was bullied on a daily basis. The abuse was often verbal, with others calling me "spastic" and similar words. However, they would also throw things at me or push me off my chair. I would wonder, "If you hate me so much, why not come and hit me? Then I could hit back." Most of the time, I was a lone wolf. I did make friends with two of my classmates, who are still friends to this day. Nevertheless I went to school every day, did my work, and got good grades—better grades than the kids who were bullying me.

At thirteen or fourteen, I started reading books about autism, and it helped me to understand the world. I have a photographic memory, and I can replay past events and conversations.

Mom adds,

If you ask Matt about a holiday, he'll recall dates, events, and anything related to it. When Matt was seven, he was reading the dictionary. Reading was his savior. He can answer almost any question, particularly if it has to do with geography. Matt studied law and criminology at the university and was taking courses toward a master's in international criminology. However, I refused to fund the rest of his master's courses because I wanted him to do voluntary work in the community and to talk with and get to know people. We were pleased when Matt did voluntary work for the National Probationary Service. We had to be firm with Matt at times.

Matt continues,

At the university things were much better. People were more respectful and didn't bother you because we were all there for the same reason. I used all my time to study. I wanted to show the world I could succeed.

My brain works like a computer and has to retrieve its responses, which is why I sometimes need time to respond. Like a computer I have a shutdown button when I get an overload. Sometimes I'm thinking about a dozen things at once. Also, I don't necessarily decipher what I hear like everyone else. If I hear someone say, "I'd like to make a toast," I get a picture in my mind of bread going into a toaster. However, at the same time, I understand the real meaning of the phrase.

Currently I am a civil servant. I handle contract management, office systems, and procedures and [do] different things every day; I am an executive officer. I take pride in making things better for people. I like to do different things every day. You don't learn a lot when you do the same thing every day. I like learning new things.

I asked Matt, "How do you reconcile the fact that many people with ASD rely on routine to manage in a world that can be confusing with your interest in doing and learning different things? Everything I've heard about autism is that strategies for supporting people with ASD usually involve structure and routine, yet you seem to thrive on change."

Matt responded,

> I've learned to handle changes in routine, and I've learned that
> change is part of life. Not everyone is as efficient and competent as
> I am, and this knowledge helps me. And even though I find whis-
> pering soothing, I can get used to some sounds."

His mom added,

> In 2015 a cousin went to New Zealand, and Matt decided he
> wanted to go. We were anxious because he would be going by him-
> self. But the three of us planned everything. Matt wanted to prove
> to us he could do it. He was gone for a full month."

Discussing his childhood, Matt's mother also told me that

> Matt struggled in secondary school, and he had difficulty sleeping
> until he was twenty-two, at which time he learned relaxation tech-
> niques while listening to ASMR videos on YouTube."

Matt continued,

> I need six hours of sleep, but throughout my childhood, I failed to
> get sufficient sleep. Then in the summer of 2009—I would have
> been twenty-two at the time—I found ASMR videos on YouTube,
> and it was then I realized how soothing it is when I hear whisper-
> ing. ASMR is the abbreviation for autonomous sensory meridian
> response.[2] These ASMR sensations had always occurred when I

---

[2] Coined in 2010, ASMR is a relaxing, often sedative sensation that begins on the scalp
and moves down the body. Also known as "brain massage," it is triggered by placid sights
and sounds such as whispers, accents, and crackles.

would hear a character in a cartoon on a TV show whispering. I suspect I had ASMR meridian response as a child, but nothing was very much known about it, so I had no idea why I experienced these sensations.

As I had no idea what I was experiencing, I didn't tell anyone about it, for fear I might be sent to a research facility of sorts. That's why I was so glad that I wasn't the only one when I saw the millions of views the videos would receive on social media. If I was born at a much later time, I think I would not have had to suffer from sleep deprivation. It is very pleasant to listen to the videos with a good pair of earphones, as it enhances the sound quality. Sometimes it does feel like the person is actually whispering to you in person.

To this day whispering is so soothing to me, and that explains why I always found solace in the school library.

Four years ago, a woman was organizing presentations for a conference, and we set up activities to help people understand how an autistic mind works. People felt our one-hour presentation was interesting, insightful, and should be mandatory.

Mom adds,

Matt is a workaholic. He has developed strategies to make life successful and enjoyable for him. Time means nothing to Matt, so he must make use of a timer. He needs gym exercise to get rid of energy. Sometimes he just walks the streets for hours—and often has no tread on his shoes due to all the walking he does. When he goes for a walk, he puts on his earphones and listens to anything from classic music to metal. On the other hand, he can burn out easily. He puts so much energy into his job that he needs to take annual leave to recharge.

Matt took it upon himself to research and explain autism to

others. He has a wonderful manager to work for in his job who will ask Matthew, "Tell me your thought process." As a civil servant, Matt is now making other staff members aware of hidden disabilities.

Matt has embraced his autism.

Chapter Eight

Supported Employment (SE) Program

When Gary developed the employment program for TEACCH, in 1989, it was without precedent. At that time nobody was thinking about the fact that autistic children grew up to become autistic adults.

Laura Klinger

It was 1989. Mike Chapman had just graduated college having majored in physics and he was working for his father in the brick masonry business when, with little background in autism, he was hired as a job coach for a one-year pilot *Supported Employment (SE) Program* for TEACCH.

Jill Keel and Amy Woods under the direction of Gary, started the program, and, together with Kathy Hearsey, the program's first director, they created employment opportunities for autistic adults. Mike became a program supervisor in 1996 and became the director in 2000 when Kathy stepped down. Mike, in his 33rd year at TEACCH, continues to direct the SE program with the help of two regional vocational coordinators, Jayson Delisle who is in his 25th year and Keri Waldrop who is in her 19th year at TEACCH.

Gary believed that adolescents and young adults could be productive employees. According to Tom Schopler,

> Dad stayed focused on little kids and their parents, while Gary was more focused on adolescents and adults. Gary wanted TEACCH to provide employment opportunities because he was concerned that there was little support for people with ASD once they got beyond their teenage years.

Catherine Faherty adds,

> Hiring people like Mike who had no experience working in the field of autism was not unique for Gary. In the early days of working on autism, there were few people who had a background of any kind in the field, so we would not look to hire people with experience. Gary would hire the person, not their background, but he would value qualities such as creativity, flexibility, and consistency. He had an ability to see people as individuals.

It was said of Desi Arnaz, the actor and producer, in the documentary *Lucy and Desi*, "He hired good men for the job and let them do it." This was certainly true of Gary.

Mike explains that

> Because it was a pilot, we began the training in four areas of the state. My only experience with autism was two weeks the previous summer when I worked at a summer camp for people with autism. It was on-the-job training. The really important thing about TEACCH was that much of the training for everyone was on the job. [Whether you were] willing to learn on the job was more important than credentials. Eric and Gary created something that has stood the test of time.

We brought all the principles of TEACCH into this program, but it was tough. In the classroom you are with the students and or clients all the time; you have a measure of control. However, with this program, you weren't with the clients when they were at their workplace. We created visuals for the employers to use with our clients and created schedules, and we helped train the employers.

Two other people were initially hired to codirect the program [Jill Keel and Amy Woods], and they published articles, as this was probably the first program of its kind in the world. This helped spread what we were doing, and eventually people were coming to Chapel Hill to see the program and inviting us to come to their state or country.

In the beginning, if we mentioned autism to perspective employers, most would ask, "Did you say 'artistic' people?" When this program was started thirty years ago, it was unknown outside of Chapel Hill, and it has grown from people knowing nothing about it to being so renowned that Gary spoke of our program all over the world and responded affirmatively to requests from people in other countries to help them get a supported employment program started. This program helped to change local/community perceptions of autism.

In the beginning our biggest challenge was to enlist employers willing to hire our ASD adults. They would tell me, "I've hired people with disabilities, and it just doesn't work out." I would say, "Have you ever worked with TEACCH? Have you ever worked with people who are autistic?"

Once they were employing our clients, it was rare that an employer didn't come back and ask for more autistic employees. Also, as evidence that all people benefit from the strategies that work with ASD people, employers often ask us to leave our visuals and scheduling materials with them to use with their other employees.

In Singapore in 2006, they were starting a school for autistic

children and wanted to develop a strong transition and employment program for the older students. They invited Gary to come
and help them, but Gary said, "There is someone better equipped
for this task," and he sent me. Others with the TEACCH philosophy also went to Singapore over the years. Singapore now has the
most impressive school-to-employment support program in all of
Southeast Asia. We got them started, and then they ran with it. I
tell people all the time, "I want to work my way out of my job."
That's my goal when I work somewhere, and that's why I am so
proud of what has happened in Singapore.

Jayson Delisle graduated from UNC with a major in sociology. He trains
individuals to be job coaches to TEACCH clients. As Jason tells his
story,

I knew I wanted to help people by doing something in human
services. As a kid one of my answers to the question, "What do you
want to do when you grow up?" was "I want to encourage people."

It is my job to make information understandable to employers.
There is such a range of things I have to discuss with employers so
they can understand how best to interact with their ASD employees. I have one person who just wants to bag groceries, and this is a
good spot for him. He just graduated high school with social skills
sufficient for being a grocery-store bagger, and he has familiarity
shopping in a grocery store and bagging his own groceries, so a
grocery store is a perfect placement for him.

Two or three months ago, I had a request from a client who
wants to be a writer. He can be nervous in social situations and
therefore not especially good in certain circumstances. I hooked
him up with a local publishing house, and he is doing well. He is
making $40,000 a year by relying on his attention to detail, his
knowledge of editing standards, and his focused attention.

There are jobs in warehouses, which are good because they have a routine and not much need for social skills. The point is that we don't establish expectations for our ASD clients, but we listen, observe, and then help them discover how their strengths and interests match the available jobs and activities in their community.

A manager may train one of our employees by saying "Here's how you can greet people" or "Here's what to say as a customer leaves." Our job coaches collaborate with the employer to individualize supervision according to the needs and strengths of the ASD employee. One of our clients is a recorded and publicized singer; he works at Kohl's department store. He is kind of large and can approach other kids with questions and scare them, so we want him to be social but to realize he needs to think about how kids perceive his interactions with them.

What's nice is that the world is starting to come to the realization that because of their strengths with numbers and their above-average ability with coding and software recognition and with many ASD people having average to above-average intelligence, they can fill the void in skilled people available to tech companies.

While awareness has increased about the skills and abilities of ASD individuals, it can be hard for corporate America to shift hiring practices and management strategies. Government-based incentives and funding [have] helped open more doors at the larger companies (and even some of the smaller ones). TEACCH has collaborated with the [North Carolina] Division of Vocational Rehabilitation (they provide funding to TEACCH) to leverage these government incentives to increase employment for our clients.

Employment does develop life skills for our ASD clients. When they are well-matched to the job, and it involves appropriate supports and supervision, there is a positive association with increased quality of life and with continued social-skills development.

Anne Haeussler, an autism specialist, consultant, and trainer in Germany who spent two years training with TEACCH in Chapel Hill in the early 1990s, describes the SE program:

TEACCH started its Supported Employment (SE) program in Chapel Hill in 1990. They offered four types of vocational settings:

- Individual placement (with a job coach)
- Dispersed enclave model (several clients at different jobs in the same business with one job coach)
- Mobile crew (stable group of four to five clients with one job coach moving and working at different locations as a cleaning crew or a gardening crew during the day)
- CLLC (TEACCH Farm), which involves chores outdoors around a farm

Anne Haeussler

Tom Galperin was twenty-two years old in 1995 and had just graduated college with a degree in social work but no real experience with autism. Having no idea what he was going to do, Tom had just moved to Raleigh and took a part-time job in a group home. There he worked with two people who were on the spectrum and part of the school SE program that Mark had designed. Tom recalls that

In 1996 I met Kathy Hearsey and was offered a job with TEACCH working with the supported employment program. Within three months I knew I was hooked on this whole autism thing, and I knew it was what I was meant to do; I fell into it backward. I was at TEACCH for nine years and have continued focusing on autism up through the present, where I have now been in private practice for the past two years.

I was drawn to this work because I had been around people with developmental disabilities all my life, even if not always autism. One of the two people I worked with at the group home had really connected with me. He was highly intelligent and yet needed so much support, sixteen hours a day, mostly because of behavioral problems. His "behavioral problems" were largely related to a lack of impulse control, a super intense attention to detail, and an inability to see others' perspectives.

Basically, it wasn't a behavioral problem; it was just that his brain worked differently. It was all directly attributable to his autism. To help him, we worked hard to establish a healthy routine, one that was predictable, one that helped make change more palatable, established concrete rules and job instructions that helped reduce the gray to accommodate his black-or-white learning style. He was also dealing with a lot of anxiety, and we worked with him on relaxation.

I asked myself, "Why would someone with so much intelligence (140 IQ) require so much support?" Then I experienced the TEACCH approach. While working for TEACCH on the SE program, I also did TEACCH training. Seeing something so effective, I said, "I want to do this." Something just clicked in me, and I said to myself, "I can do this; I can be good at this." And I enjoyed it, and I enjoyed and respected the people I was working with. It felt like home to me. That feeling of family was all Gary's doing. The search for core values through surveying staff and then the adoption of them has helped me even after I left TEACCH. I have used the core values many times throughout my career.

So much of what we used as selling points to employers were strength-based:

- They could be trained in a routine and would stay with it.
- They love coming to work because it is part of their routine, and that is important to them.
- They rarely take vacation time because that is not part of their routine.
- Similarly they want to come into work even when sick.
- They don't take fifteen minutes on a five-minute break because to them, five minutes means five minutes.
- They won't steal.
- They don't waste time gossiping around the water cooler.

I got the foregoing from employers and then used it to sell potential employers. Employers would tell me that they will gladly take the extra time to train our employees in a routine because it would save them a lot of time dealing with problems they would have with their other employees.

Tom stayed with TEACCH for nine years before he went back to graduate school to become a social worker.

Lee Marcus explains that

> The relationship between the TEACCH Center and Supported Employment was a close one. Most centers did not have their own program but would refer adults they evaluated to the statewide SE program. There was a connection among all the different programs and aspects of TEACCH; no matter what you were working on, you needed to know all the other aspects."

Here are some anecdotes about the work of the cleaning crew at Gary and Laurie's home. This first one is told by Christina Corsello, North Carolina, director of clinical services, UNC TEACCH:

> Among the job opportunities for our clients was the opportunity to clean houses regularly every week or two weeks. The houses for cleaning belonged to staff, friends, or parents who volunteered, and one of these houses was Gary and Laurie's. As part of the SE program, Gary had asked Mike to develop, a mobile crew of four autistic people and a job coach would go to homes to clean. They did a really nice job, but they often shared what was happening in everyone's home. For example, Gary used to tell me how they would tell everyone that Gary has so many books everywhere, and they are so dusty, and that they had to clean them all.

These next two are told by Sloane Burgess, professor, Kent State University, and a TEACCH trainer in Ohio:

- One of the cleaners was vacuuming a bright white carpet in the Mesibovs' home when the belt broke, spewing dirt in a straight line from one end of the carpet to the other. Intent on finishing the job, the cleaner continued to push the vacuum over the line of dirt until the entire white carpet was no longer white and ultimately had to be replaced.

- Another time a cleaner was at the house when the kitchen was being remodeled. Asked later if he had noticed the remodeling that was underway, he replied, "Oh, yes, Laurie's shoes were in a different place, one of the chairs was angled in a different direction, and the table had been moved to the other side of the room."

I love their attention to detail—they can have such an eye for the slightest detail.

Chapter Nine

Social-Skills Groups

Groups of ten would often break into smaller
groups, and each would act out a social situation—
what to do and what not to do.

Cathy Lord

It a is a no-brainer that if a trait common to many people with ASD is
a lack of social skills, then helping them improve these skills should be a
focus of their preparation for life. Yet until Gary put a spotlight on social
skills, this was largely ignored by professionals in the field.

According to Mary Beth Van Bourgondien, "another major contribution of Gary's to the TEACCH program was his development of services
for adolescents and adults with autism and their families, starting with
social-skills groups."

David Moser previously explained that "Gary got us all together, and
this helped me find my best friends through these social groups."

Andy Short says,

Gary had a depth of his commitment to the families; this was a
great strength of the program. And Gary had a nice way of working with autistic people on their social skills. He created what could

almost be called a social club, through which staff could work on social skills by making it fun. He taught kids how to understand social cues and to tell jokes and stories."

Barry Prizant is director of childhood communications and services in Cranston, Rhode Island, and has written several books on autism since completing his doctoral work in the mid-seventies at the State University of New York in Buffalo. Barry remembers, "I attended a TEACCH Christmas party in Chapel Hill in 1990, and one-third of the attendees were adults with ASD. It was the first time I had ever met so many people with ASD in one place. I walked in the door, and they asked us to put on name tags, so mine said 'Barry Prizant, Cranston.' I was quickly approached by a young man who, after reading my tag, told me, 'Oh, you live in Rhode Island; the highest peak is Jerimoth Hill.'"

Barry Prizant

Jayson Delisle told me,

> Gary would come to social groups at fun outings at the park or for overnight stays, and he would come and be so accessible, you wouldn't know he was a psychologist. The autistic clients loved him. He had understanding and compassion and was so great to work with.

He would get with a group of five autistic people, and this could be tough because they would each be fixed on a different agenda and be demanding of his immediate attention. He would start with one and pay rapt attention but move quickly among the five, giving each his undivided attention before circling back to the first one. He was very personal.

We would hold large-group social functions with thirty to forty people with ASD and another ten support providers. We had many responsibilities, and so we had many ways to put a foot in a mouth. I was nervous initially in these large groups because I wasn't sure how to interact 'appropriately.'

Gary knew the interests of all the clients and all the trainers, so he paired us by interests. I was paired with Jeffrey, who loved nature and specifically trees, and I liked the outdoors. More than twenty years later, we still go hiking together. Jeffrey's in-depth knowledge of trees inspired me and opened my eyes to the vast differences in fauna and flora. Before I just saw the forest, but now I see and appreciate the details—and the trees. He has had a profound effect on my life.

Eleven years after Gary first paired us, I joined Jeff and his Sierra Club for a hike in the mountains. We drove four hours. When we started out, it was a warm, comfortable day. We met with his club, changed vehicles, and now, we were passengers in another vehicle. When we got above 3,000 feet, the sky darkened, and the temperature quickly dropped into the twenties. It was sleeting. The road got icy. The car skidded into a barrier and overturned and landed overlooking a long drop off the side. I had to talk Jeff through each of twenty steps to get him out of the car: "Take off your seat belt; now put your foot on the headrest (confusing since that's where he usually puts his head), climb up through the window, step out, and put your foot on the roof rack. And now…"

When we are finally in a new, warm car with someone who

picked us up, Jeff starts talking to the driver about the trees we had seen and a variety of facts, not about the wreck we just experienced. He had completely moved on.

Cathy Lord first worked with someone with autism in 1969 and met Gary in 1976. Between 1990 and 1994, Cathy helped establish the Greensboro-High Point Autism Center in North Carolina. Cathy has focused on autism in Ann Arbor, Michigan; Chicago, Illinois; New York City; and Edmonton, Canada, frequently visiting Chapel Hill to conduct TEACCH training. She is currently the George Tarjan Distinguished Professor of Psychiatry and Education at UCLA. According to Cathy,

> Gary set up social groups in Chapel Hill, which I replicated in Greensboro. These social groups would meet regularly, sometimes weekly. They would include people with autism along with graduate students and with friends and/or staff. There would be ten to a group.
>
> The groups of ten would often break into smaller groups, and each would act out a social situation—what to do and what not to do. It was fun, particularly when a few people would act out what not to do. They might act out a situation involving appropriate etiquette at the dinner table or how much food you should take when filling your plates or whether to reach across someone when wanting salt or pepper. We would pick out typical situations that might cause people with autism difficulty.
>
> What distinguished Gary's social groups was that some would go on forever—twenty years or more. Other programs might continue for up to fifteen weeks, but with TEACCH, while staff, friends, or grads would move in and out of these groups, some of the people with autism would stay for many years. This was important because those with autism often do not develop friendships easily. Spending a long time with the same people nourished the development of friendships.

In these social groups, the people who were not autistic acted as group members, not as therapists. Over the years I attended several Thanksgiving dinners with Gary, Laurie, and their sons, Brian and Todd. Gary just lived his values. He would invite young adults with autism to Thanksgiving dinner at his home.

One of the times I was there, we were joined by three young adults. They were excited, thrilled to be with us. They really worked hard to be on their best behaviors. They had definite ideas about what they would or would not eat. One of the three wanted everything that was on the table. He had never seen so much food at one meal. He loaded his plate with some of everything. We were afraid he would feel he had to eat everything on his plate and would get sick.

Another one of the three was obsessed with the curtains being open. He wanted them closed. It really bothered him. We didn't want to be trainers at Thanksgiving dinner, but we did ask him how this was important to him and whether it would be appropriate for him to ask the homeowners to close the curtains.

Being in someone's house was unique for all three and important to them. We enjoyed it too.

I learned this from Gary: On the one hand, we are taught to be professionals at all times and to set up boundaries and adhere to them. But Gary taught me there needs to be flexibility. To invite autistic young adults who rarely had occasion to visit anyone else in their home was OK on a special occasion like Thanksgiving, where the purpose was to give them a unique experience. This was not a violation of the distance a professional should maintain from a patient. Gary did not engage in inviting his patients to his home throughout the year. A one-time exception was OK even though many professionals would say, "Don't ever invite a patient to your home."

Actually, inviting people with autism to his home on

Thanksgiving was an exception. Gary had created social groups, and this exception was consistent with his efforts to teach social skills to people with autism by putting them in situations, thus giving trainers a chance to model appropriate social skills in an environment where the clients could practice them.

Where do you draw the line? Gary was clear in his own mind where to draw the line; he knew when to be flexible and when to hold fast to an established boundary.

Cory Shulman says of her experience with social groups,

I believed the social groups Gary created and TEACCH promotes to be so important that I followed Gary around for about three weeks one summer (1995). I remember Gary's commitment to the participants, and some really good ideas emerged. Once we took a trip to the library and used the library system to teach the importance of keeping things organized and putting things back where they belong. I came back from that meeting with the following mantra: "Everything has a place. Once you find it, keep it."

Brigitte Nelles is a psychologist clinician in France who says,

TEACCH is part of my whole career. I met Eric Schopler at a conference in Paris in 1985 and first met Gary in 1986 while attending TEACCH training in Belgium. When Gary came to the airport to pick me up, a person with ASD often came with him. Gary had promised someone that he could accompany us to the airport when I was scheduled to return to France. He got so excited, he asked Gary if he could invite someone to join us. Gary said, "Yes, it's your decision, but remember you don't like to be tight in a car, and Brigitte will sit in the front seat because she is our guest." Well, the person with ASD invited two friends and then complained throughout the entire ride that the car was too crowded.

Signe Naftel has been working for TEACCH since 2003. In 2010 Signe developed an online curriculum for autistic adults to find and keep a job. She says,

> I would take out clients with autism who needed enrichment. There was one very special adult man with curiosities that had to be addressed. I took him to all sorts of libraries—public, university, other—to meet his interests. Our adult residents often loved outings of any kind. For instance, some wanted fancy dinners. Gary would take them to fine-dining restaurants like Il Palio in the Siena Hotel, a AAA Four Diamond restaurant. When I took them out, I took them to Chick-fil-A or a similar fast-food establishment.[3]
>
> Gary always went above and beyond. He treated them like family. He also took them to coffee shops (not ordering anything with caffeine) and did these types of things.
>
> A unique part of TEACCH, and Gary in particular, was that while most autism centers focused on kids, Gary did, too, but he also focused on fostering services for adults. He had a vested interest in not just children but adults. TEACCH was also unique at the time by having supports for employment not readily available elsewhere.

Joanne Quinn says,

> We have thirty-one social-skills groups with six to a group plus a minimum of three staff, which include professionals who know

---

[3] Gary and Signe paid from their pockets, not an expense account. This might not be possible now due to regulations.

how to start the group members talking. The older ones may have as many as twelve in a group. The lower-level people with autism need one-to-one supervision in their groups. They often need to take a break or walk outside. Tweeners learn how to hang out with each other.

Kelly Trier has been an autism consultant and advanced TEACCH trainer in Iowa until her retirement this year, having begun her career in 1985. Kelly recalls,

I trained as a speech-language pathologist, and in my first job, I had five different schools with the toughest kids in the city to work with. I fell in love with my job and loved working with a couple of the kids that had autism spectrum disorder who were struggling, and that is how I ended up looking for more strategies to help and advance my training so that I could help others.

My best memories of Gary Mesibov, after getting over the fact that I was in a room working with one of the biggest names in autism, were in his respectful way of honoring individuals with autism. I learned from Gary about how important it was to offer the individuals with autism the opportunity to share their interests, challenges, hopes, and dreams with people who came to learn.

The first trainings that I went to at Chapel Hill, Thursday nights, were always when adults with ASD would join all of the participants from TEACCH at dinner. Gary would have the people with ASD share about themselves with the tables where they sat; it was an honor to have these wonderful individuals with all of us and to see them as the guests of honor at the dinners.

That is how it felt as an outsider looking in. Gary was able to explain why people with autism do the things that they do in a respectful and understandable way, in which he could change a person's perspective from one of not understanding the unusual behaviors seen to one of complete respect for how difficult it must be to try to fit into a neurotypical world. Just knowing why ASD people do what they do changes people's perspective of them. Gary used this as an opportunity to honor individuals with ASD.

Bernadette "Det" Dekeukeleire and her husband Peter were among the Belgian pioneers who, led by Theo Peeters, were responsible for TEACCH's first venture in Belgium, which in turn led to TEACCH spreading throughout Europe and, eventually, almost the entire world. As Peter tells the story,

In 1986, Det joined Gary and his work with social-skills groups in Chapel Hill. The Chapel Hill social-skills groups usually numbered about six young adults, with some staff members, doing social activities like going to a restaurant. Det copied the model and translated it to a Belgian context.

Bernadette "Det" Dekeukeleire and her dog Yoko

Det picks up the story, continuing,

> I still have pictures of a Friday evening social group in Chapel Hill in 1986. I went to dinner with Gary and some of the autistic people with whom he was working. Over here in Belgium, we call these social get-togethers "bridge activities" because they are a bridge between people with autism and non-autistic people.
>
> We work primarily with those on the spectrum who need substantial support, because it is not easy for them to participate in mainstream free-time, sports, or cultural activities. We provide activities that go beyond social-skills training; they include psychoeducation, cultural excursions, science, or sport activities, playing games, cooking, or other enjoyable cultural things. We send out invitations to around 150 people with autism, and depending on the nature and location of the activity, we usually get fifteen to twenty-five participants on each activity."

Vickie Shea has collaborated with Gary as cowriters of published articles beginning in the 1970s and culminating with the writing of their book about TEACCH in 2005. Vickie says,

> Gary often invited young adults to Duke or North Carolina basketball games if he knew this was their interest and believed they could handle the noise. Tickets were hard to come by, but Gary used his connections to obtain them. On Thanksgivings Gary would invite colleagues and their wives and sometimes young adults with ASD as well as unattached staff. I went maybe ten times. Laurie often invited people also."

Before Jayson Delisle's long-term pairing with Jeffrey, he was paired with another person who loved the outdoors and who, like Jayson, loved to hike. As Jayson relates the story,

We hiked through Umstead State Park, six adult clients and two staff members including me. It was a two-mile loop. We lost one of the six adults.

We got to the end of the walk, and all of a sudden, someone said, "Where is he?" He had sneaked off somewhere along the way. He was highly intelligent and could be verbal but rarely spoke to people, in fact just didn't like to speak much. He also liked to hide, so I had visions of not being able to locate him.

I'm thinking, "I will lose my job." I was scared, really scared. "I'm definitely going to lose my job." Finally, after a search by the park ranger and others, we located him. Now we are in the car. I am glad he is back, but I am also so mad. "Victor,'" I said in a loud voice, "What the hell were you doing?"

Very calmly Victor replied, "I was going to come back."

Of course due to his autism, he had trouble understanding another person's perspective, and he just assumed everyone else knew he planned to come back.

Chapter Ten

Strategies for People with ASD

If a child isn't using something in a positive way, don't extinguish their interest; change it slowly and make use of it.

Keith Lovett, quoting Gary

There are many and varied strategies for providing support to people with ASD and their families. But the starting point is to get inside the person's head, understand how the person perceives the world, and then determine how to effectively communicate with the person.

Kelli Bielang is an engagement specialist with Kalamazoo County, Michigan. She is also a certified TEACCH trainer. Kelli believes,

The whole point of teaching is to engage students in instruction.

Unfortunately, too many teachers in "regular" classrooms try to teach through lectures, and while this may help auditory learners get good grades by memorizing information for tests, it fails to teach them to think critically. Consequently, many students whose learning styles are more visual or kinesthetic than auditory have difficulty engaging with what the teacher is saying.

Jennifer Townsend is an educational consultant with Universal Access Consulting, LLC; her expertise includes social-emotional learning differences. Jen, whose most recent book is *Think Differently: An Educator's Approach to Appreciate What Works,* says,

> Reading is left to right, so a work system should be the same. I remember Gary's passion when saying, "It has to be left to right." So you start at the left, where you set up the work and where the person can see how many tasks he has to accomplish. In the middle put what you are working on. The least amount of prompting takes place in the middle. Students work as independently as possible. A structured system can be set up anywhere: in a phone, portfolio, binder, folder, device, Google Calendar, bookshelf. You can set it up anywhere.
>
> Sometimes we set up a strategy spontaneously. A student dropped his backpack on the floor, and everything was a mess. I set up a hook for his backpack. I set up three baskets: one for a lunch box, one for his school materials, and one for trash. Now when he comes home, he takes his lunch box to the kitchen and throws out his trash and then starts his work system. The family thought I was a miracle worker.

Toni Flowers' career includes being a director of special education supervising autism programs in Indiana, and being honored as the 1989 Autism Society of America teacher of the year. Toni currently teaches children with autism in the Indianapolis Public Schools where she stresses the importance of the work stations.

> In the early 90s, I came to Chapel Hill for the five-day TEACCH training, and that just changed everything I knew about autism; it all came together for me.

For instance, I learned that workstations for people with ASD are critical. The stations define what to do, how much to do, what it will look like, and when the student will know they are finished.

I learned the left-to-right strategy and that you must be certain a student can do the work independently before you move them into the workstation. Recently a new student only needed one day before he understood the workstation. We can take a workstation into an inclusionary setting and modify it so it blends into other students' work.

We also do a lot of one-on-one work. There are certain activities students need to do to prepare them for using workstations. We look at the very young children and ask, "What will they need when they leave school?" So from the very beginning, we stress working independently. We have strips with every student's name, and we label them "in progress" or "independent." We monitor to see when they are ready to move into independent workstations.

Examples—Can they:

- complete an almost-finished puzzle?
- take paper/pencil tests?
- put beads on pipe cleaners?
- do fine-motor activities?
- do housekeeping tasks such as folding a basket of scarves in a pile?
- fold or sort socks and put [them] in the "finished" basket?

Kara Hume is a TEACCH trainer/associate professor in North Carolina and has worked in Arizona as well. She reflects,

I always knew I wanted to be in the field of special education. I went to a Catholic high school, and as part of service learning, which I had to do, I worked with a young boy with autism when I was sixteen. It was an in-home program. I learned how to connect with people other than through verbal language by paying attention to his body language and cues, and I learned how to appreciate his strengths and interests.

Svany says,

Gary was so right when he said while I was working with a difficult population, "Stay with them. It will come to them; it will come to you." He would say, "Pause; wait until they calm down and you are calm, too. How to deal with someone in a difficult situation will come to you. Stay calm." Today we call this coregulation.

I would pause for a while, stay calm, have them sense that my belief is that they are able to say, show, or otherwise indicate so that I can understand what they want to communicate; so I wait and of course provide pictures, words, or written follow-through by waiting and expecting a response.

As Svany spoke, I reflected on what I've learned from experts about how to address problems with students who are upset or being disruptive; they often recommend exactly what Svany is suggesting, except this advice relates to dealing with anyone who is upset whether they are ASD, or not, and whether it is an infant throwing a tantrum or a high school student behaving poorly.

Quiet is empowering to people with autism. Stay with them in silence and quiet, and that will empower them. People with ASD are so sensitive to our way of being; if we're stressed, they will be stressed. So pause and get on the same page that they are on. Their antennae will sense your attitude and your state of mind—not what you are thinking, but what you think of them; they know if you do not accept them.

Keith Lovett, England, director of Autism Independent UK, related what Gary would often say:

"Use what kids like, and gradually modify it to move the child into areas you want the child to progress to."

For instance, Keith explains,

If the child likes mushy stuff, like dough, let him play with dough but then show him how to make pancakes, and gradually, you may encourage him to wash some of the dishes so he can use them again to make more pancakes. The end result is the food or snack.

If a child isn't using something in a positive way, don't extinguish their interest; change it slowly and make use of it. So if a child likes to play with string or water, find constructive ways they can use it. Always answer the questions the child may have before they ask them. For instance:

- What am I doing?
- How long do I do it for?
- What do I do when I am finished?

Work from the schedule with line drawing, tactile, pictures and or written et cetera. So [the answer to] "What am I doing?" might be matching pieces into pairs from a group of pieces, randomly displayed.

"How long do I do it for?" Until all the pieces are gone, until all the pieces are off the table and matched.

"What am I going to do when I am finished?" You will get the piece of fruit that you like, or you will get to play with a piece of string for five minutes, or you will...

Keep things very simple, try to answer questions before they are asked, i.e. "What's in the parcel?" Leave a present partially open, showing part of something the child likes.

Gary would say, "If you are going to do something or go somewhere, you need to plan it with precision. For example, show pictures of the house, then the places you might walk or a picture of the car you will drive in (or of the keys for the car), then the store that is your destination. But think this through, because once you share it, you need to stick to it. If the picture of the store has green curtains, but the curtains are now red, the child with autism may get upset or confused."

Before TEACCH most schools had a special-education teacher who didn't have the right tools to teach children with autism. Gary trained professionals to teach autistic children life skills, how to learn, and how to give these children more understanding. The main thing was to give people with autism communication skills well beyond spoken language.

Gary helped change perceptions, change education—not called "treatment"—and change approaches to training. The implication of the word "treatment" is that they are ill and will get better. If you don't put structure in their lives, they will make their own structure, and it may not be what you want. This is analogous to "[Idle hands are the] devil['s] playthings," only there is less room for error with an autistic person. However, once they or you put a structure in place, it becomes like cement and is very hard to remove.

This last statement brought to mind a story Alice Wertheimer told about the tutor from Tennessee's first meeting with her son David.

On her first day with David, the tutor held up a large card with the word "red" printed on it. In her deep southern accent, she said to David, "I want you to repeat after me," and she proceeded to say, "ray-ed." So David repeated, "ray-ed." David is now past forty years of age, but according to Alice, the color red is still "ray-ed" to David, thus illustrating that once a person with ASD learns something, it becomes, as Keith explained, "like cement" and very hard to remove.

Keith continues,

Gary was called into a school, and the headmaster was proud of a teacher who had pretty good control of the class while she was in the room. Gary noticed that when the teacher was out of the room, all hell would break loose. So he told the headmistress, "You need a structure that isn't dependent on the teacher being in the room because the teacher isn't always going to be in the same place with the child."

Someone in the audience asked if this was a good teacher. Gary responded, "She may be a good teacher, but she has a problem."

Gary would also say, "You don't really understand autism if you do two or more things with the student at the same time. It can contribute to overload and be confusing." He pointed out that it is necessary to avoid

- touching the child
- putting your eyes close to the child's and making eye contact
- trying to explain or instruct through speaking, or
- having too many things going on at the same time; too much distraction

Gary urges people to "Keep a low profile with distractions at a minimum; take one thing at a time; use visuals. Some classes even will have windows blacked out to limit distractions."

Susan Moreno illustrates effective strategies as follows:

At our conferences we have stickers for people with autism: a red sticker means 'Don't approach me'; a yellow sticker, 'Approach me with caution'/'I may not want to shake hands'; and a green sticker, 'OK to approach me." Susan adds that there are rules at her conferences, including "no strong perfume," "no smoking," and "no touching or handshakes." We also have panels that include people with autism.

Joanne Phillips was Arizona state director of special education from 2003 to 2007, and she used the opportunity to make a statewide impact. Joanne started an autism initiative with Svany as the coordinator. Joanne tells of an experience she had in 1975 when as a student at Hofstra University in New York State she was doing some work at Maimonides, a private school as part of a program her mentor/professor set up:

A girl I believed to be severely autistic entered my therapy room one morning. I looked up at her as she entered, and I sang, "Good morning." She sang back, "Good morning." This was the first ver-balization we had ever heard from her. She was clearly hearing me, processing the melody in the right brain, but the language process-ing finally made it to the left brain. Words without melody couldn't get through to her left-brain language center.

Simply put, there is a bridge between left and right brain which we all have called a corpus callosum. It allows input to be processed and relayed to both sides of the brain. When we see something from one eye, the brain sends that signal to its other side so both eyes can recognize it. When she heard music, the right brain picked up the music and sent the words via the corpus collosum to the left brain for processing. She wasn't just mimicking me; she was processing what she was hearing. The words made sense because of the music.

She made considerable progress, and then I was able to diminish the melody as time went by. That's when I knew I wanted a career in autism. I knew from this experience that autism had to be neurological, genetic. You couldn't force them to learn; you had to earn their trust.

I had to ask for permission to use melodic intonation therapy, which at that time was developed for aphasic patients. It required approval from the principal at the time, and fortunately, [it] was given.

My next clinical practicum was in Northport at the VA hospital in New York, where I actually used the melodic intonation therapy (MIT) with aphasic patients who had sustained stroke damage on the left brain. This made making language understanding and formation difficult, but again, using MIT to overcome the neurological issue, progress was seen.

Nathalie Plante, a teacher and now a TEACCH certified advanced consultant, has infused the province of Quebec, Canada, with the principles of TEACCH. Nathalie went to Chapel Hill with three trainers from Quebec for the five-day training sequence. Nathalie relates that,

Kids about five with autism had many needs. Many were hyperactive and couldn't sit still for a minute. We tried to make schedules for them with pictorials, but these were too abstract for them. They needed objects. For example, instead of just seeing a picture of a pencil, they needed to be shown or handed an actual pencil. The first thing we made was a physical structure for them. Providing a schedule worked for some of them, but not all. We saw the need to organize and prepare for increased diagnoses.

Cathy Pratt says,

> Lee Marcus came to Indiana, and along with me, we did TEACCH training. We did make one modification to improve the training. We used to spend weekends setting up classrooms. A lot of trainees would ask us, "How did you set it up, and why did you set it up that way?"
>
> So we shifted the setting-up of classrooms to Monday and Tuesday, and as part of their training, the trainees would set up the classrooms on those days under our coaching, and then we would bring the students in for the last three days instead of all five as we had previously been doing.

David Preece tells us,

> TEACCH principles have long been a given in the UK and many other countries. For example, in the UK's Department for Education and Skills (2002) publication "ASD: Good Practice Guidance—Pointers to Good Practice," many of the indicators of good practice are derived from TEACCH:
>
> • Account has been taken of the need to create a low-distraction workplace within the classroom setting (for example, the creation of a workstation-style area) and a clearly defined space for personal equipment and belongings.
> • Clear signs/symbols/photographs are in evidence in school communal areas and subject bases.
> • The school has taken account of the vulnerability of some children with ASD to environmental distraction in terms of acoustics, smells, and lighting (for example, use of daylight tubes in classrooms).

- Teachers provide visual clues for the child in the form of time-tables, key subject words, and language.
- Lesson plans are written up in such a way that a child can check where they are up to.
- Visual timetables are placed at the right height for the child.

David says, "All of this is pure TEACCH."

Kelly Trier says there are a lot of stories that she has from TEACCH trainings while she was working as a trainer at UNC at Chapel Hill, and these are a few of her favorites:

On the last day of our five-day training, we would always take our students out into the community in some way to show how to expand the structure of TEACCH to the community. On this particular Friday, I was working with a student who did not do well with initiating conversations and did not make phone calls on his own. Initiating communication is a difficult area for a lot of individuals. This particular young man was supposed to be initiating a phone call to someone who was driving the van that would be going up to and from a bowling alley. The child needed to know how to make a phone call in case the need arose.

I made out a script for him, and it went something like this: "Hi, this is James. I am at a bowling alley, and I need a ride. If no one answers, then hang up, wait five minutes, and call again." The first time we rehearsed, he read the entire script including "If no one answers, then hang up, wait five minutes, and call again." I had to add quotation marks around the words he was to speak. People with ASD tend to be literal. It amazed me that all we had to do to make this work for this young man was to move the quotations to what he was supposed to say and highlight those words, and he was able to make the call himself. He just needed the script of what to say in the situation and needed it printed out with quotes to help him to follow it.

Another time we tried to teach a person with ASD how to introduce himself to someone. He would get really close to someone and would say, "Hi!" I taught him to stand at arm's length by holding my arms outstretched to show him the distance between him and me. However, when he tried to rehearse it, he also held up his arms to measure the distance between him and the other person. I put into his visual the imaginary arm's length distance, and we practiced that. So his visual looked something like this:

Greetings when approaching people:

> Walk to the person
> Stop about an arm's length distance
> Say "Hi _____"

This young man had brilliant academic skills for his age but was so overwhelmed with anxiety in social settings that just saying "Hi" was completely overwhelming to him. The visuals I learned how to create at TEACCH helped him to gain this skill.

Kelly adds,

My job can be stressful, but when people see how the strategies work, and they use them, that's what gives me satisfaction. It always feels good to know you've made a difference and you can see you are making a difference. What I love most is helping others to see that they can make a difference in the life of a person with ASD. The principles of TEACCH start with learning about autism and how it impacts individuals, then learning about the physical structure of the environment, the use of work systems, and [the] visual structure.

The most impactful strategies for most of my students are the individualized schedule and the work system. These two strategies can be adapted in so many ways for whatever a child's needs are. I have had the opportunity to help put together everything from a carry-and-use schedule to a check-off printed schedule to a texture-flip-book schedule for a visually impaired student.

What these two levels of structure provide [are] a way to know what is happening in your day and, for each location you are transitioning to, it provides clarification on these four questions that often are hard for people with autism to understand:

- What they have to do
- How much they have to do
- When they'll be finished
- What comes next

In 2010 the city of Cedar Rapids, Iowa was flooded, and over 4,000 homes were underwater. It was June, and I had to go to TEACCH training in Chapel Hill in July. I was working with a mother who had twins, each with ASD and each significantly autistic. They were seventeen at the time.

One of the twins was so stressed, she was pulling out her hair. I said I would watch her during the day (my home was not affected). Her mom, a widow, was having a challenging time explaining to this twin why she could not go back to her home and why they had to stay with friends. At my suggestion Mom took her to their house so she could see why they couldn't return at this time.

This seventeen-year-old with autism made a work system (a to-do list) for her mother. She said, "Mom, you need to get the mud out of the house and clear the clutter from the kitchen; you need to put away the things on the floor in the living room; you need to…" She listed out for her mother the things that needed to be done to the house, and it gave Mom a way to show her what was done, what still needed to be finished, and how long it would be before the family could move back to their home.

TEACCH strategies gave this young lady a way to handle an extremely stressful situation. I shared this story with Gary and the team of trainers as I cried for the first time about all that had happened to our city and how a strategy made such a big difference in an otherwise stressful situation.

Vickie Shea explains intervention strategies called "Structured Teaching":

An example is that if a parent is having difficulty with a child's behavior from the time school lets out until dinnertime, a structured-teaching strategy might be to suggest something the parent could do to engage the child during those hours. The specific activity would depend on what the parent knows about the child's interests.

Catherine Davies says succinctly,

Many of these stories illustrate strategies for supporting people with autism. For example, unless you put up visuals on how to make a bed, they will be doing things at forty they were doing as a child. "

I would add that if that if the person was taught as a child that the color red is "ray-ed," the person may still be calling it "ray-ed" at age forty.

Chapter Eleven

Strategies for Students with ASD Are Best Practices for All Students

The world of education would be a better place if everyone learned strategies for coping with autism and then used them wherever they ended up.

Cory Shulman

David Preece has stated, "It is important to teach in the learner's principle modality, and for most of us [not solely for those with ASD] that is not auditory." The disconnect in the way some teachers approach student learning in "regular" classrooms is that too many rely primarily on strategies for auditory learners. They ignore the significant number of students who learn visually or kinesthetically; and this begs the question of whether preaching to auditory learners and asking them to regurgitate on tests what they have memorized in any way challenges them to think critically even if it does enable them to get high test scores.

While conducting interviews for this book, a special day for me was February 23, 2022, because that was the day I had lengthy Zooms with TEACCH trainers Kelli Bielang and Katie Bozarth. Each provides instructional support to teachers: Kelli for all of Kalamazoo County in Michigan and Katie for her school in Washington, DC. They coach the teachers on their staffs, particularly, if not exclusively, with regard to working with students with special needs.

This was a special day because these two teachers, ironically, were coincidentally scheduled for Zooms with me the same morning, and they are unique among the eighty-three people with whom I have been speaking. While each is a certified TEACCH trainer, they are the only K-12 teachers with whom I conversed who are currently working in schools. At the time we spoke, Katie was in her eighth year of teaching and Kelli in her twelfth.

Both Katie and Kelli have been mentored primarily by Kathy Hearsey and each is laudatory when speaking of Kathy.

In addition to being the only people I interviewed who are working full time in "regular" schools, neither has ever had personal contact with either Gary or Eric. This is significant because it means that the principles of TEACCH are continuing to guide a new generation of practitioners, and this is what I believe to be the mark of success: when something you start is institutionalized to the point where it continues after you depart. I founded the Institute for Learning Centered Education in 1995, but to this day, despite concerted efforts, I have been unable to hand off the vision and application to others, so I admire Eric, Gary, and the people at TEACCH for succeeding where I have not.

It is nice for the ego when you believe that something will be unable to continue without you; however, it is far more meaningful when it can. Eric Schopler acknowledged this as he approached life after retirement as TEACCH director in 1993. He was quoted by his son Tom as having said, "I fear that TEACCH may not survive without me; however, I also fear that it might."

Katie proclaims,

> I came to TEACCH for training in Chapel Hill three times, the
> most recent being March 2019. Each of these times, I couldn't wait

to return to my school and try out what I was learning. I worked a lot with Kathy when I was in Chapel Hill and by phone when I was working to qualify as a TEACCH trainer. Kathy is wonderful.

In addition to providing evidence that the principles of TEACCH are surviving the departure of Gary and Eric, and will survive the departure of anyone else who retires, there is another reason that speaking with Katie and Kelli was so meaningful. They along with others have validated my observation that the classroom strategies essential for supporting people with ASD are also best practices for all students.

Cory Shulman told me, "I once said that the world of education would be a better place if everyone learned strategies for coping with autism and then used them wherever they ended up."

I would add that the best training we could provide for regular classroom teachers and future teachers would be to prepare them to teach people with autism. If you learn the strategies that are absolutely essential for working with people with ASD, then you also have a complete repertoire for teaching anything to anyone.

Katie's Story

Katie Bozarth

Katie Bozarth is a coach, supporting all twenty-five teachers at her Washington, DC, school. Katie says,

> I first became interested in autism in middle school. When my peers and I would leave the cafeteria, I would see numerous older students (whom I later found out had autism) come behind us to wipe the tables and clean up. This upset my sense of justice; I remember thinking how unfair this was. Then I learned that this was one of several vocational jobs these students had.
>
> I was raised on the Eastern Shore of Maryland, so it was a huge adjustment when I began teaching in DC. My students all had a range of cognitive impairments, autism being one of them, and I immediately learned so much. I didn't realize some of the strategies I was learning to implement at the time were actually principles of TEACCH. For instance, the task can be changed over time so the student can master new skills, but overall the left-to-right structure remains consistent. This is critical for students with ASD since often, they are unable to judge what the end of a task will look like, and this can be frustrating.
>
> I began teaching at my school in 2015. Two years later I went for the five-day training in Chapel Hill. I had been approached and encouraged by the leadership of my school to go for the training, or I might not have gone—I was not secure enough in my teaching ability at that time and was unaware there was an opportunity like this available to me. At the training I learned so much more about how children with autism take in and process information. I learned they can be overwhelmed by too much information, particularly verbal directions. I was able to understand so much more of the "why" behind some of the things I had already been doing in my classroom.
>
> After returning from the training, I had the opportunity to implement many of the strategies I learned in North Carolina. These approaches were effective with all my students, not just the ones

with autism. I experienced many small successes and saw growth in all my students.

As the instructional support teacher, I ask teachers to:

- look at physical boundaries in the classroom
- think about the different types of individual schedules your students might use to independently transition throughout the school day (objects for concrete learners, pictures, pictures and words, words)
- consider parent training—what is transferable that we do from the classroom to the home such as schedules, visual supports, materials
- view all behaviors as communication—what is the student trying to tell you?
- keep an open mind and try to look at the situation through the autism lens

When I meet with teachers, we work together to structure tasks that will address each of their students' IEP goals. I have an exercise where I will put an unclear task in front of them and ask them to complete the task. When the teachers struggle to complete the task because they are unsure of the purpose, I ask them to imagine what this is like for our autistic learners.

When I am called in by a teacher, it is usually because of frustration due to a problem behavior they are experiencing with a student in their classroom. Teachers are spread thin with all the responsibilities and duties they need to address during the day. Many of our students:

- are not toilet trained and need to be changed on the changing table, which takes two staff members
- are fed by G-tube; some have vision impairments (cortical visual impairments)

- have seizures
- have complex communication needs (a majority)

And the list goes on. All of these additional responsibilities require specialized training. It can be overwhelming and exhausting trying to manage all of this in addition to instruction.

We are in a year-round school, as many of our students would not be able to retain information if they had a typical summer break. Many of our students with autism work in the community, and we have partnerships with different community organizations around DC. We work hard to prepare students to be ready to go into the community with as much independence as possible by the time they are twenty-two. We have social groups, and we try to teach them to appreciate jokes—their favorites are usually knock-knock jokes. Even if the joke is corny, we all still appreciate a good laugh.

The principles I've learned from TEACCH have absolutely shaped me into the educator and coach I am today. I live for the aha moments when a teacher I am supporting makes a connection or has success after implementing something new.

Kelli's Story

Kelli Bielang

Kelli Bieland supports teachers throughout Kalamazoo County. Kelli says,

> What is exciting is that teachers come to my workshops to learn strategies for dealing with the few ASD students in their classrooms, but they realize that these strategies are effective with all their students.
>
> I was initially hired as a special-education teacher for students with ASD in Kalamazoo County, Michigan, and now my title is engagement specialist for the Kalamazoo Regional Education Service Agency (KRESA). I work with various districts in the county where KRESA provides educational programs and services. I coach teachers in special-education and general classrooms how to use evidence-based supports/interventions. Most of the professional development I provide is related to autism. KRESA has multiple classrooms kindergarten through twelfth grade for students with autism throughout the county.
>
> Students attend these classrooms when they need more specialized ASD programs and services. The program's goal is to send them back to their home district/school with the ability to learn in a general-education classroom with their school's special-education programming. In 2018 two professional TEACCH trainers did training here at KRESA. From this the TEACCH principles continued to build. It is now an administrative vision to implement Structured Teaching. We are expected to use TEACCH methodologies.
>
> Our data shows students are able to make progress with these systems and supports in a less restrictive setting. The reason my title is "engagement specialist" is that the whole point of teaching is to engage the students for instruction. I coach educational stakeholders [on] how to use evidence-based supports/interventions that benefit all students.

I had had some TEACCH training in my prior district, so I was already using it. Our data is now showing that students with autism that are accessing TEACCH/Structured Teaching are returning to their home schools faster."

I have attended multiple TEACCH trainings in North Carolina. Special-education administrators are supporting the implementation of TEACCH/Structured Teaching throughout the county. We take a strengths-based approach. If you're using these practices, you're hitting everyone. As I said previously, regular classroom teachers are not seeing this as something just for students with Individualized Education Plans (IEPs). It's about knowing your audience and using Structured Teaching as defined by TEACCH. Teachers need to be flexible and take the students from where they are to move them forward.

I really love the work I am doing and knowing what the outcomes will be for our students. I'm still learning how to make it work even better. Witnessing students' responses to positive outcomes and seeing them self-regulate and feel good about themselves motivates me to keep going.

I am a firm believer that all kids can learn if they see meaning, and it's our job to help them find meaning.

I asked Kelli, "How do you work with students to help them develop a sense of humor?" She responded,

I set aside time in my classes to help students learn social skills; having a sense of humor is a part of having social skills. I find that peer-to-peer coaching is more productive than what I could do. I don't know what's in the mind of a twelve-year-old, but other twelve-year-olds do. I provide the lead with a question—it could be "Why is this joke funny?"—or I provide them with social situations to learn, and then, having provided a hypothetical situation, I let the partners discuss it.

In a high school classroom, a student might tell jokes in a monotone voice. With this and other aspects of socializing, I will provide the lead but let the teaching and learning occur through the peer-to-peer discussions. Also, I use areas of interest to bring peers together; perhaps two students share an interest in SpongeBob.

Catherine Davies says,

A somewhat unexpected outcome of our work with people with autism on a grant was that since the grant required implementation in both special and general education classrooms, we were able to observe the strategies successfully supporting neurotypical students and those with disabilities other than autism. One middle school assistant principal told me that if I would have previously told her to use a visual support when students were sent to her for discipline, she would have thought it was crazy, but it turns out it was much more effective than the previous methods she had been using.

Echoing what Cory Shulman had said to me, Toni Flowers tells people,

You may not continue working with people with ASD, but what you will learn, you can use anywhere.

Catherine Faherty recalls that a kindergarten teacher who was to have one student with autism the following September had participated in the week-long TEACCH training, and afterward, she said, "I am so excited. I am going to use these strategies in all my classes."

Lore Gray, a teacher in Rhode Island, and cofounder of the Autism Project, reminds us, What works with autism works with everyone. But not everything that works in regular classrooms works with autism. Our work with TEACCH training has spread to many classrooms in Rhode Island. Regular classroom teachers would come to our presentations when they had children with autism in their classes, and they'd realize they can use the same strategies with their own students that work successfully with students with ASD.

Marie Howley says,

> The key to Structured Teaching was to show how this approach could be used to teach different curricula in England for all students.

Fukuda Toshiyuki, Japan, a journalist and photographer, reports,

> Now many people in Japan know that people with autism can learn visually, even children in regular schools.

David Preece adds,

> Do we expect ASD people to internalize? It's not just ASD kids who need all these visuals in the classroom. Many nonauditory learners also benefit from visual aids. We all like it. In Japan I travelled with pictures of a bathroom, restaurant, drink, et cetera so I could function visually in a land where I didn't know the language. This way I could approach anyone in the street and ask my questions. Instead of written travel guides or in addition to them, someone should publish a photograph guidebook.

What if a person with ASD is also blind?

As has been cited throughout this book, experts on autism stress the impor-tance of using visuals with people on the spectrum. There is little hope of supporting ASD people with auditory approaches to learning. They learn best visually and physically. But what if in addition to being ASD they are also blind, in which case the learning must be almost exclusively physical.

David Preece and Marie Howley describe how strategies have to be ad-justed for people with ASD who are not visual and this, of course, includes those who are blind. In an article, 2003, entitled *Structured Teaching for People Who are Visually Impaired* the authors ask,

> What is the main difference between people with ASD and other people?"

They respond to their own question, saying,

> What people with ASD need is an outside structured environment. There are certain things they can't internalize like the rest of us. You need to put in external structure for them. You need to make the intrinsic tangible. My wife, Kim Taylor, is a teacher of deaf and blind children. In 2009 we presented our work at several interna-tional conferences in England and the United States.
>
> How do you adapt visuals to the physical environment using the other senses? You use wet, dry, soft, hard; different textures; dif-ferent materials. These strategies work as well with nonvisual and visual learners.

Kelly Trier sums up the universal application of strategies for people with ASD, saying,

> We must make sure there are strategies for all students, not just

students with ASD. Much of my work is in observations and training staff. We have found that TEACCH strategies work for all kids and can be used in all classrooms. There are teachers out there that are putting the structures of TEACCH in place in their general-education classrooms for all their kids to be successful. The visual structure that they add allows for their classrooms to run smoother and to increase the predictability, routine, and independence of the whole classroom.

Many teachers teach the way they were taught: for auditory learners. Depending on the teacher the use of visuals in a classroom can vary from extensive to very little. And because most teachers will not experience having to teach students who are blind, very few teachers have received training in the use of physical strategies to enhance learning.

However, there are many people whose best learning modality is visual or physical, and a teacher whose repertoire includes strategies for auditory, visual, *and* physical learners is prepared to teach all students, not just the auditory learners. Therefore, teachers who learn strategies for addressing the needs of people with autism are prepared to teach all students.

Chapter Twelve

Around the World with TEACCH

> TEACCH principles are now a given in most countries. I've done training in Croatia, Macedonia, Poland, and Spain. TEACCH underpins practice across all of Europe."
>
> David Preece

Part One: England and Japan

I had intended to relate the influence of TEACCH in every country where TEACCH trainers have worked. However, I discovered TEACCH has conducted trainings in so many states and countries, it is not possible to share all that people have to say about the status of supportive services and the impact of TEACCH in their geographic locality. According to the program's 2020–2021 annual report, TEACCH trainers visited 42 countries and forty-six states in the United States during the previous year. Many of these countries and states have been receiving TEACCH training and turnkeying it since before 2000. Therefore, rather than attempt to report on each of these countries and states, here are descriptions representative of the impact of TEACCH around the world.

Probably the most captivating stories are of Gary's connections with

Russia and Saudi Arabia, and you'll find these stories later in this chapter. However, initially I am going to focus on England and Japan because of the numerous times Gary, Eric, and other TEACCH trainers conducted sessions in these countries and how their work in these countries ultimately spread to other places on their continents. Then we'll explore the role of TEACCH in some of the other countries and states where its principles and practices have become a foundation for information and support in the field of autism.

Here are a few examples of the pervasiveness of the program that Eric and Gary developed and that TEACCH trainers, presenters, and other devotees have gradually spread to six continents:

Mary Beth Van Bourgondien has made multiple visits to Argentina, Australia, Belgium, Denmark, England, Germany, New Zealand, Northern Ireland, Scotland, Spain, and Sweden as well as Colorado, Illinois, Massachusetts, New Mexico, New York, North Dakota, Oregon, Tennessee, and Virginia. Lee Marcus has conducted training for TEACCH in Belgium, Bermuda, Canada, China, Germany, Greece, Israel, New Zealand, Slovenia, Sweden, and Switzerland. Laurie Sperry is an autism forensics and criminal investigation/clinic director and founder of autism services and programs. Laurie's TEACCH resume includes work in Colorado, Hawaii, Africa, Australia, India, Saudi Arabia, and Singapore. Many other TEACCH trainers have worked in multiple states and countries. And of course many have worked extensively in North Carolina.

The list could go on. Trainers often make repeat visits, such as Svany, who works in Arizona as a TEACCH trainer but returns annually to Iceland, where she has established a reputation for helping build the country's autism support system. Gary visited England twice a year for thirty-one years, Eric opened the door for TEACCH in Japan and visited there many times, and Gary went to Japan annually for approximately forty years to conduct training and make presentations. Let's begin with England and Japan and then explore some of the many countries and states where TEACCH helped educate people about autism.

England

Citing some of the history of autism in England, Marie Howley told me,

In 1989 the late educational psychologist Terry Arnold and his wife, Eileen Arnold, speech-language therapist, and social worker David Preece were sent to the United States as a multidisciplinary team to explore approaches to autism and to recommend an approach to introduce in Northamptonshire. When they came to division TEACCH at Chapel Hill and met Gary and other TEACCH colleagues, they said, "This is what we need to take back." At their invitation Gary came to England and would sit in on classes. He loved to be with students, and students loved him.

Gary came to Northamptonshire in the 1990s. I was new, enthusiastic, and keen to learn, and I was one of the first in England to be trained by him. He was very supportive. Gary was just amazing. I attended the first TEACCH seminar, led by Gary, in Kettering, Northamptonshire, the very first TEACCH training in the country. I then attended the first TEACCH hands-on workshops, also in Kettering, and subsequently became a TEACCH trainer whilst teaching in a special school. Gary would visit my classroom with friendly advice and suggestions. Later he would recommend teachers visit my classroom as a model of Structured Teaching; as a result I had a lot of visitors to my class!

The use of video material of teachers and students and staff working in a classroom setting was immensely important because no one in the UK had seen this type of demonstration before. This was the power of visual learning.

In 1999 I left teaching in special schools (although I continued as a TEACCH trainer) to become a university lecturer at the University of Northampton. I was trying to make the leap from schoolteacher to lecturer on autism at the university, and Gary sent me all kinds of lectures, papers, and relevant information. At this time I was invited by Gary to be a TEACCH trainer at Chapel Hill and then to stay on and research university curricula [that] focused on teaching undergraduate and postgraduate autism programs. Gary would always encourage trainers from overseas to come to Chapel Hill as TEACCH trainers. My husband and three year old twins came with me. Gary was so kind and friendly to my family.

In 2001 as the United Kingdom accumulated a growing number of experienced professionals, teachers, speech-language therapists, social workers, and the like, Gary suggested we try to replicate the in-service training event that took place annually at Chapel Hill. Consequently Gary and I set up the first TEACCH international conference at the University of Northampton to provide further opportunities for experienced professionals to reflect and enhance their practice and to share their research. The event was to be a professional conference where we would bring people together from England and throughout Europe. Parents of children with autism were also invited, in line with the principle of including parents as coworkers alongside professionals.

Gary was mindful that there were a growing number of people who could share their expertise. The conference took place biannually until 2013 with around three hundred delegates from around Europe. The conference still runs at the University of Northampton as an Autism Study Day.

Gary approached me in the early 2000s about writing a book on the National Curriculum because he was getting questions from our schools about children with autism. We had started implementing Structured Teaching in special schools, but now we were getting more and more questions from mainstream schools, where educators wanted to know, "How can we teach the National Curriculum to make understanding of autism more accessible—which the law requires us to do? We have to follow the National Curriculum." We talked at length to identify the key purpose of a book. "How can we use Structured Teaching to enable children with autism in special and mainstream schools to access the National Curriculum in a meaningful way?"

In 2003 Gary and I coauthored *Accessing the Curriculum for Pupils with Autistic Spectrum Disorders*; our purpose was to demonstrate that strategies for addressing the needs of students with autism could be integrated into the National Curriculum in England without the need to create an extra curriculum or extra work for teachers.

After our book was published, I then spent many years speaking at conferences about the content. As time went by, others in Europe became interested, and we were asked to write a second edition, which Signe Naftel helped edit in 2016.

What was it like collaborating with Gary on the book? We worked out a structure in terms of who would do what and then made many phone calls. I'm smiling as I recall this because I would email my chapters and then wait ages for Gary, who would FedEx hard copies of what he was working on. My children, twins aged six at the time, knew Gary through his visits here when we would work together. They would see the FedEx truck outside and yell, "It's Gary's book."

In 2011 Gary was awarded an honorary doctorate at the University of Northampton in recognition of the significant contribution he had made to autism services and education in Northamptonshire. Gary was extremely happy and loved the doctorate gown and especially the cap. In an email I later sent to him, I said, "Your honorary doctorate was awarded for your amazing autism work with us in Northamptonshire. We had a lovely day—I remember you joking about and liking the cap."

I once asked Gary, "What do you do when people keep asking the same questions?" His response, logically enough, was, "I give the same answers. If it's the right answer, I keep giving it, but I find different ways of saying it."

Marie Howley with Gary, 1911: "Gary loved the cap"

David Preece speaks with pride, saying,

> In England and elsewhere, TEACCH underpins everything. TEACCH principles are now a given in most countries. Back in the 1990s, these were still considered new strategies and a new approach and a strange thing that people were doing; now it is accepted practice.
>
> I first met Gary in 1994 when I was running services for children with disabilities in the county of Northamptonshire. My work included children with autism—there were very few at that time, but services we were running for others were not working well for people with ASD.
>
> We started the Autism Project, and we wanted something that was not too invasive, meaning we wanted something that acknowledged and respected the people with autism rather than attempting to make the child with autism "not autistic" (as ABA did with the use of aversive techniques). TEACCH accepted the autism and worked on the environment, the physical structure, et cetera, and

making expectations concrete via schedules, work systems, et cetera, rather than using verbal/physical prompts [or] getting in the space of the child with autism.

Then we heard about Project TEACCH. Terry Arnold had come back from visiting TEACCH in 1992. Our initial reaction was, "Oh, yeah, we'll take this wonderful thing from America." Terry spoke of Eric Schopler and others. The TEACCH approach seemed much less invasive and intrusive and felt more appropriate and respectful.

Eventually I went into this class in Kettering where Project TEACCH was being employed, and this girl who was usually all over the place (*arms waving chaotically to demonstrate*) was working calmly. So I said, "Maybe there is something in this." And I met this very calm, very unassuming gentleman, and I could not believe the amount of time and kind of attention he gave me. I went to Chapel Hill, and I worked closely with Gary and then returned to England.

Project TEACCH and Gary impacted thousands of professionals over the years. Gary had respect for others no matter how many times he was asked the same questions. Gary gave of his time generously. He was also interested in how we were providing services in England and was really helpful with services development. He did consultations with classroom teachers. He helped us develop the Arnold House, named after Terry, which is a children's home. Terry had passed suddenly in 2004.

Gary didn't want us to make the same mistakes he and his colleagues had made in the earliest times with TEACCH, so he shared with us their mistakes so we could avoid them. He came around to see a children's home we had built that wasn't working that great. It was really helpful to have this person whom my higher-ups really respected help me get them to support our ideas at a time when they preferred to be cutting expenses.

Gary was really motivating for all of us. It was impressive that he could focus so much time on us while he was simultaneously writing books, publishing articles, editing journals, supervising student interns, and directing TEACCH. With all this he was still hands on, working in classrooms, with social groups, and with the people who were taking advantage of his research and experiences. Staying active in the field enabled Gary, when people would invariably ask, "When were you last doing this yourself?" to say, "Just last week I was in such and such place."

Not that many academics keep in touch with the clinical side. My colleagues respected him. If they had kids with ASD with them, Gary demonstrated he knew just what to do to connect with them. He was always out there, and he loved being with these people—the kids and their families.

We tried to pick his brain when he would come over. "OK, Gary, we tried this, and it doesn't seem to be working."

Gary would say, "Hmmm, I wonder why that is?" He never exhibited any defensiveness. He might say, "OK, that's what I didn't expect to happen, but let's figure out why."

Keith Lovett spoke with me about his son born with autism in 1983 and his experiences working with Gary and TEACCH:

When my son was born, I closed my businesses and resolved I would spend ten years learning about autism and taking care of my son. From 1983–1987 I looked after my son and looked for direction. My son was diagnosed at age three, but we suspected something was wrong when he was two.

In 1987 I founded and became director of the Society for the Autistically Handicapped (SFTAH). The name was later changed to Autism Independent UK because it wasn't accurate to label autism a handicap. I had been calling experts from around the world, and that's how I came to find Gary. In 1989 someone referred me to Gary, and I made a transatlantic phone call to him. It had been very difficult to get information about autism in England. There was one international publication, not very helpful. I telephoned Gary and asked, "Could you come over to England?" He said yes. I asked him, "How do we pay?" and he said, "Don't worry about it; we will look at that later."

On his first visit, he was greeted with a large crowd in the main ballroom at a local hotel. Professionals, parents, and anyone with an interest in autism were starved for information, for someone to address their questions.

Gary returned twice a year for thirty-one years, even the last three years when he was obviously in a lot of pain from a worsening condition that severely limited his ability to walk. But he told me, "I won't let you down; I will be there." And he was, right up until COVID 2020, when everyone's travel was limited.

Even before he arrived for his first presentation, Gary sent us information and referred us to the books he and Eric were writing. Over the years he would give us permission to copy and distribute many of his writings, I think to the dismay of his publishers. Ninety-nine percent of the people at subsequent trainings were new because schools, universities, care divisions, and psychology departments would send many new staff to be trained to work with autistic students.

I would put Gary up in a separate hotel from all the other guests and participants because they wouldn't have given him a moment of privacy and would have besieged him with questions on sight. Some of the higher-ups from other organizations would try to steal him away from us, but Gary would tell them, "I committed myself to this organization." Gary was honest, fair, and loyal in all of the dealings I had with him over thirty-one years. He got his start with parent organizations, and he never forgot that. He was also a product of routine—same foods, same hotel, same approaches to teaching.

I gave Gary a five-year calendar so he wouldn't forget his commitment to us. And we paid him two or three years in advance. He brought a lot of money back to the TEACCH program from his international travels over the years.

Gary really changed the entire way training was done and autism was approached throughout the United Kingdom. Many in the United Kingdom jumped on the bandwagon, and many trainers and publishers tried to copy him and take credit for his methods, but it was Gary who changed the entire way the UK approached autism.

Gary has created an entire industry in the UK and around the world. Other countries sent people to evaluate what Gary was doing, and then even when Gary wasn't here, we would get requests to train people in other countries with what we had learned from him. Our training with Gary provided a springboard for many other countries to take up the training program.

Steve Love adds,

A woman in England left her school and went to another and brought us in to train there. Evidence of our success in England and some of these other places is in the length of time we worked there, indicating they were satisfied with our work and kept inviting us back.

Eileen Arnold says, understandably,

It is a shame Terry is no longer here to share his experiences of Gary with you. Terry was the main mover and shaker who first contacted Gary and worked tirelessly to get things going in Northamptonshire. When Terry and I first met Eric Schopler, he said, 'speech pathologist and educational psychologist—the dream team for autism." We tried to live up to that!"

Japan

Interpreter Kay Shigematsu with Gary

Gary's frequent interpreter Kay Shigematsu says,

> There was a child psychiatrist, Dr. Masami Sasaki, who was the main driver in introducing TEACCH to Japan, and he passed away a few years ago. Dr. Sasaki was a real good person who wanted the best information possible about autism in Japan. Around 1980 Noriyuki Fujii, known as Nori, who runs a company that organizes tours and seminars, introduced Dr. Sasaki to the TEACCH Program. Nori was also instrumental in future years in bringing Gary to Japan.

In the late 90s Sasaki summarized his connection with TEACCH in a letter he wrote to Eric Schopler supplied by Brenda Danzler:

The first time I came to North Carolina was in the summer of 1982 with ten colleagues. We stayed for only five days in Chapel Hill at that time. We were nevertheless so impressed and excited to learn the beautiful, total, and comprehensive program of treatment and education for people with autism in North Carolina, when we were just in the face of difficulties as to how to give our people with autism and their families some hope and courage for the future.

Dr. Schopler and his TEACCH staff gave us well prepared, excellent lectures and took us to some facilities, group homes, sheltered workshops, and so on. We deepened our understanding of the real nature of autistic disorders and the adequate treatment and education of autistic people. I will never forget the strength of the TEACCH staff's friendship; it moved us a great deal.

On getting back to my country, I introduced the TEACCH principles and methods on the bulletin of the Autism Society of Japan. And then Mr. Fugii and I held the first and second TEACCH Training Seminars in the summers of 1983 and 1984 with kind cooperation of Dr. and Mrs. Schopler. In a few years, the name TEACCH became popular among almost all people working for the autistic in our country.

Then we opened more TEACCH seminars in the large cities of various districts of our country in partnership with Drs. Schopler, Mesibov, and their staff colleagues.

Dr. Schopler, meanwhile, continued to give me his kind suggestion that the training of schoolteachers was of overriding importance to develop TEACCH methods in my country. So, in parallel with these lecture seminars, for a four year period we were able to have TEACCH TRAINING SEMINARS (sic) for schoolteachers and other professionals in our country, by calling on TEACCH staffs from North Carolina to give the actual trainings to Japanese trainees."

And thus began Gary's annual August trips to Japan. Interpreter Kay Shigematsu tells of how the connection with Gary and TEACCH grew:

In 1995 Nori asked me to go to Europe with him and a small group to visit France and Denmark. He had already been to Chapel Hill and wanted to learn more about the status of autism services in Europe. After that Nori asked me to translate every time anyone came over, usually Gary, Kathy, Mary Beth, or Lee.

In order to translate, I thought it would be better to learn more about TEACCH myself, so I went to Chapel Hill with Dr. Sasaki and kept returning annually almost to the present, sometimes alone, sometimes with a small group, and often with Tomoko.

Kay talks about the admiration people in Japan hold for Gary:

In Japan people loved him. Every time after a lecture, he'd be surrounded by people with questions and comments, and if it was a full-day lecture, I would have to pull him away to get lunch. Whether it was a lecture, workshop, or conference, he was always surrounded by more people than any other presenter. I think that is because he listens and responds, and that attracts people. Also, Gary remembers people whom he met in previous years when he returns each year. Our people are very appreciative of that. "Oh, Gary recognized me."

When people experience Gary, Eric, Kathy, Mary Beth, Lee, or anyone from TEACCH, they learn to value them and the TEACCH principles.

Gary is very good at time management. He would always stay within the allotted time and still have enough time for questions. This is important because of the need people with ASD have for routine and for relying on something to end when they have been informed it would end. If the ending time was supposed to be 3:00 p.m., they wouldn't understand if it didn't end at that time, whether the reason was more questions to be asked or a speaker who had more information to share or whatever the reason.

Gary's last visit to Kumamoto, Japan on Aug 31, 2018. He was hosted by the Autism Society of Kumamoto. Left to right, back row are Kayoko "Kay" Shigematsu, Mr. Matsumura, Mr. Sakaguchi, Dr. Kyoko Tanaka, Dr. Okada. Front row: Dr. Gary Mesibov, Dr. Steve Kroupa

Kay proudly states,

Tomoko did her internship with TEACCH in 1992-1993 in Chapel Hill. She returned to Japan, and that's when I started interpreting for TEACCH. Elementary schools can be too visually stimulating. Elementary school teachers need to learn how to set up the environment and not to rely on spoken language too often.

Tomoko adds:

I use Structured Teaching. I credit Eric and Gary for bringing TEAACCH principles to Japan, and this has led to considerable changes. I am head of the Japanese TEACCH Certified Professional Network, and Gary is on the board. On his visits Gary travels from one end of Japan to the other, from the large island of Hokkaido in the North to the island of Okinawa in the South. His stops include Hakodate, Sapporo, Kyoko, Osaka, Hiroshima, and many other cities in Japan.

Tomoko was my main contact in Japan; she suggested some of the people I interviewed. She says that

> In 1989 I was a participant in the conference during Gary's second visit to Japan. I presented my case study to Eric and Gary, and they offered me very positive feedback. That may be one of the reasons I was offered a scholarship to visit Chapel Hill; Gary was my guardian. I actually worked for a year at the Asheville TEACCH Center, returning to Chapel Hill every Friday to visit the Social Club and work employment program, both of which were fantastic.
>
> Gary was such a role model. The people with autism loved to meet with Gary, you could tell. And, as I said, he spent his personal time with them, which is what I am doing in Japan. After that first time, I visited Chapel Hill once a year for the May TEACCH three-day conference, which was moved to October in 2012.
>
> I became one of the organizers of the Japan annual conference. In 2002 I started inviting Gary to my one-day conference in Northern Japan in addition to the two-day conference he attended every year. He was responsible for a lot of changes in how Japan viewed autism. Gary continued coming to Japan for our annual conferences for forty years. On days off I brought him to Hot Springs and sightseeing with my colleagues.
>
> At the turn of the century, people thought autism was a severe, untreatable disability. His preaching helped us. Gary told us

this: "Autistic people are not less than others. Autistic people are not retarded. They just have a different way of seeing the world, and it is our job to help them make sense of the world."

I found Gary fascinating. There was a mix of people each year when Gary would address our conferences—people from previous years would return, and they would bring with them many new people. Japan has been heavily influenced by TEACCH. I translated *The TEACCH Approach* into Japanese, and it sells well.

David Preece says,

TEACCH was already in use in Japan when I visited there in 2003. I was invited over by Tomoko and had the opportunity to visit autism facilities throughout Japan. While there I visited a number of services that were based upon the TEACCH model. These ranged from classrooms to adult day care facilities. I visited a shiitake mushroom farm that ran on TEACCH principles—from growing to packaging, a restaurant, and a local bakery.

In Japan professionals were almost worshipful of TEACCH, in particular Eric Schopler and Gary. In the training trainees would observe students in the classroom and then would discuss with the trainer what they saw. At the end of a session, I would ask how they felt about what they had observed, and they would all bow.

Kyoko Tanaka says that when she and Steve Kroupa first met in 2005, it was common for professionals from around the world, especially from Japan, to come to Chapel Hill for TEACCH training. Steve says,

The Japanese contingent first came to Chapel Hill in the late 1980s, and TEACCH appeared to work so well that they thought it was magic. Up until then they didn't have many strategies that were working well. Also, TEACCH fit in well because it was so structured, and having structure and routines is part of the Japanese culture. Also, the Japanese people seem to have a well-developed ability for processing visual information, so the use of visuals makes a lot of sense to them.

Kyoko adds that

TEACCH's initial success was largely because of the Japanese experts who learned about the TEACCH approach and began educating others in Japan. These early experts were very enthusiastic about TEACCH. One of Gary's attributes that made him so successful in Japan is that he was an enthusiastic teacher who was good at explaining complex concepts. Gary used easy words and was good with metaphors, and he understood the differences between our cultures. Eric and then Gary were so easy to understand and friendly to the Japanese; they both made a real effort to understand and respect our culture, and this, along with their warm personalities, made them welcome in Japan.

Eric and Gary were both very friendly and kind to everyone. They were both always smiling and seeming to enjoy meeting people and doing what they came here to do. Gary's view of the world was to respect people with or without autism, respect everyone. In Japanese culture it is very important to respect everyone. He and Eric modeled respect for everyone, and that helped others to treat people with ASD respectfully.

Steve adds,

I always enjoyed listening to Gary because he was very knowledgeable, presented his ideas in an interesting way, and he had a good sense of humor. His warmth and friendliness come through across cultures, and maybe this is what endeared him to the Japanese people.

Being associated with TEACCH brought instant credibility and respect by many in Japan. For example, about thirty or forty parents and professionals would come to North Carolina from Japan each year. Once I was giving a lecture to this group, and after my lecture, an elderly woman and a younger colleague who served as her translator came up to me to express her appreciation for my talk, adding that I was a kind man, and she would like to be my wife. It is quite possible that I misunderstood what the older woman was saying, and something was lost in the translation, but this story suggests the "status" that being associated with TEACCH held by some in Japan.

Just the affiliation with TEACCH made us into very important people to some in Japan. Eric helped pave the way, but Gary created his own place. We were treated like royalty. We were frequently treated to dinners at nice restaurants, and important people in Japan would be there. There would be speeches, and invariably there would be expressions of how much they appreciated our support. This was an important way to spread ideas.

Kyoko Tanaka is currently working in a psychiatric hospital for people with serious disabilities and behavioral problems. This includes working with people with autism and their families. Kyoko says,

I appreciate working with these people and they appreciate me. I incorporate TEACCH in everything I do.

Mike Chapman has conducted trainings in Japan and Singapore, and he recalls,

One of the great things in Japan is that they have integrated TEACCH into their culture as well as their training. For instance,

in many countries, they copy literature about TEACCH principles exactly as it has been written for people in the United States.
However, in Japan, they have rewritten the TEACCH principles to
recognize how Japanese culture will interpret them. They will call
us and say, "This doesn't make sense in Japan if we take it literally.
Let's discuss it and see if we can figure out how to interpret this for
Japanese people since our culture is different. Oh, that's what you
mean."

They wouldn't just translate word for word. They would partner with us in translating what was written for an English-speaking
audience to what will be understood by people in the Japanese
culture.

Sally Mesibov went on a trip to Japan with Gary in 2016, and Gary's wife,
Laurie, accompanied them. Sally recalls,

Thinking this might be Gary's last trip to Japan, I had asked, "The
next time you go, can I come with you? I really didn't expect him
to say yes, but Laurie asked, "Are you serious?" She hadn't gone
on previous trips, knowing Gary would be working. However, the
chance to go and have someone to be with while Gary was busy
was appealing to her.

The Japanese loved Gary. They all wanted to have their pictures taken with him. They called him "Typhoon Gary" because
August was the start of their typhoon season, and Gary and the
first typhoon seemed to arrive at about the same time every year.
The hospitality in Japan was unbeatable—unlike anywhere I have
ever been. The people are always happy to help. I think Gary's approach to his training was very professional and similar to how he
approached everything—he always seemed to put the needs and
desires of others first.

Fukuka Toshiyuki with Gary on Shinkansen. First-class cars on Japan Rail (JR) lines are called Green Cars. They are found on shinkansen (bullet trains) and tokkyu (limited express trains). Because standards are so high on Japanese trains, even the ordinary cars are usually sufficient.

Fukuda Toshiyuki says,

> In 1980 everyone in Japan was confused about autism, and we didn't understand what it was or how to work with people who are autistic. The 1989 training in Japan with TEACCH was the start of bringing change to Japan on how we think about autism. We had invited four people from TEACCH to come to Japan, and Gary, Kaia, Kathy, and one other person came and did the five-day training. I shot the videos of them doing the training, which included videos of them working with children in classrooms.

As the training began, we were very shocked to realize we were doing things all wrong.

> We had thought people with autism were self-indulgent, and we learned this is not true. We couldn't understand their circumstances, and we were working the wrong way. We didn't realize

they just see things differently from us. We were very surprised to see the people from TEACCH doing some of the things they did with our autistic children.

Since then much has changed, and I have gone to North Carolina for training four or five times. Between 1990 and 1994, I worked closely with Gary and produced videos of his lectures during the five-day training. In the early nineties, I sent about six interns to Chapel Hill to work with Gary. Tomoko was the first person I sent in 1992, and subsequently, I would send four or five people a year.

When I first worked with Gary, I couldn't always understand what he would say, and he couldn't always understand what I would say—just like with autistic people. We must understand autistic people in order to provide services for them and their families. It's a matter of human rights, and in the 1980s, we didn't have human rights for people with autism—not even now in many cases.

Gary would say that people with autism need people around them who like them and care about them. This can help people with ASD to have a perspective on what their life may be like as they grow older so they can start early in life to work on the skills they will need to gain employment and have fulfillment later in life.

Many people can't understand that people with autism are visual learners. We should thank Gary for teaching us that. There have been big changes and now you will find people with autism in the schools, whereas that was not the case in the 1980s. We now have centers for autistic people in every prefecture in Japan. In 2004 when I invited Gary to Japan, over one thousand people came to hear him speak. After that he came every year at my invitation until 2018. We did conferences nineteen times with Gary here. People came from all over the world—professionals, parents, doctors, university students, institute staff.

In 2016 my wife, daughter, and I went to Gary and Laurie's home for a Thanksgiving dinner. I remember the turkey and all kinds of cakes. Todd took us to a basketball game at Duke University. Also, in 2016 when Laurie and their daughter-in-law Sally came to Japan, they witnessed the esteem in which Gary was held by the Japanese people. Laurie said, "Wow, is he famous; I didn't realize how famous he is." I told her he [was] famous not only in Japan but all over the world. She was surprised.

I miss Laurie very much. Gary made his last trip to Japan in 2018, having previously had to cancel one trip due to surgery. No one can do a lecture like Gary. He is very clear and easy to understand. I produce videotapes all over Japan, the United Kingdom, and Australia, all over the world. But Gary is the best. Everyone loved Gary. He taught us about TEACCH.

Tokio Uchiyama is one of the most esteemed authorities on autism in Japan. He recently wrote to me,

> I represent the TEACCH Society Japan. I decided on this English name about twenty years ago in consultation with Gary. Let me give you a little introduction to the society. The first TEACCH leadership training seminar, held in Japan in 1989, led to the creation of TEACCH society Japan, headed by the late Dr. Masami Sasaki. Our society was a small group with less than ten members at the start but has now grown to a group of 1,800 members.
>
> I think the reason why the association has developed in this way is because Gary and other TEACCH staff have been supporting us for a long time. It consists of twenty chapters across the country, from Hokkaido in the north to Kagoshima in the south. The main activities organized by the head office are the biannual Collaboration Seminar (lectures and practical reports by invited

lecturers from the TEACCH Department in the United States), the Practical Research Conference held in February/March, training seminars, and the publication of the journal *Purau*. Also, each branch holds its own regular branch meetings, lectures, and conferences. Seminars and other activities unique to the branch are actively developed.

Dr. Gary has made a huge contribution to autistic people, parents, and supporters in Japan. There are a lot of autistic people and their parents who love and thank Gary. We are very grateful to Gary.

Part Two: Around the World with TEACCH

Africa

Joanne Quinn, Rhode Island, told me that,

> We have, ourselves, now done TEACCH training in Africa, Ottawa, South Africa, and Seoul Korea.

In 2019 Laurie Sperry spent a month in Namibia helping teachers structure their classrooms. Namibia is a diamond-mining town—well resourced, however." According to Laurie,

> They wanted to learn a lot more about dealing with students with disabilities in their own classrooms. We helped them work in their own classrooms using positive behavior intervention supports to change the dynamic from a punishment to a positive paradigm. We worked with teachers on positive interventions and student learning. First, use strategies to prevent problems. When problems do occur, let's step back and see what we can do to avoid the same situations happening again.

Australia

Sam Brassington, Perth, Australia; special needs educator/leader and TEACCH certified practitioner. told us,

> In 2003 I applied for a VIF (Visiting International Faculty), which placed people in certain US states for two to three years. I was posted to North Carolina and started teaching in a small, rural town, Lillington.
>
> I began the TEACCH five-day training course at Greensboro in July 2004. The first day it all seemed so logical. Think of people with autism as just thinking differently. It was the best training I ever had in my twenty-five-year career. The fact that you could discuss concepts in the morning and actually put them into practice with people with autism in the afternoon made the training worthwhile. It was also helpful that TEACCH leaders would observe me in the classroom and advise. I have taught and used the TEACCH principles and structures throughout my career. I loved the philosophy of the culture of autism—not trying to change anything, just to improve the quality of life.
>
> Other teachers in Australia would watch what I was doing and then do the same. It was wonderful doing here in Australia what we had been doing in North Carolina and seeing it work so well. It is so nice when kids understand the expectations and know what they have to do with no stress and no anxiety. The principal asked me to write down what I was doing so she would have it for training new teachers.
>
> Gary came to Perth in 2013. Compass Australia, a private company, arranged his visit. There were other cities he visited, like Melbourne and Sydney. The saying that "autism is not a processing error; it is just a different operating system" was one of the things I recall Gary saying. It sums up so well the philosophy of TEACCH and respecting the culture of autism. TEACCH is very well respected around the world.

Laurie Sperry was in Australia from 2010 to 2012 and reports,

> I had gotten a Fulbright and worked in Australia, and my job was to establish an early childhood center in rural, out-of-the-way areas. I created a center of excellence and used the hub and spokes process I had learned in Chapel Hill. You establish a center of excellence and bring people in, train them, and have them go back to their own center with consultation and support from the center of excellence; you build additional sites in rural, remote, underserved areas supported by the center of excellence.
>
> Everything was about trying to build capacity: teaching other people to go back to their own areas and use TEACCH principles.

Louise Loosen is a special-needs teacher in Western Australia and says,

> I first became aware of Autism during my teacher training in 1996. We received a one-hour lecture on autism for the whole degree. My next experience was when I moved to the UK in 1998 and commenced a teaching role at a residential school for students with ASD. I was enrolled in a TEACCH course presented by Gary and Kathy in Kettering, Northamptonshire, UK, in 1999.
>
> TEACCH has supported practitioners to move away from a deficit view of ASD to a whole-person view. TEACCH has supported the movement toward a wraparound support approach and the acknowledgment that a person with ASD is a lifelong learner.

Belgium

The TEACCH odyssey that would ultimately reach six continents began its journey from Chapel Hill in Belgium after a man named Theo Peeters visited the TEACH program in 1985. This was discussed earlier, in chapter four, so I will simply highlight a few aspects of the TEACCH connection to Belgium.

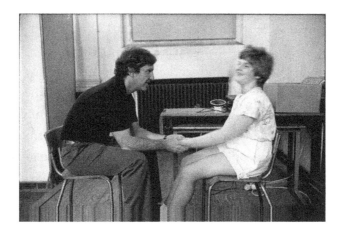

Gary with an autistic girl named Sandra during the TEACCH
practical training Gary did in Antwerp, Belgium, in 1986.

According to Peter Vermeulen,

There was nothing in Belgium to support people with autism or their families when we started in 1982. Only Theo Peeters and the parental society were doing anything. Now there is so much about autism in every book, newspaper, magazine—autism is well known in Belgium now.

It's not perfect. You still have to wait on long lines for some of the services, and the unemployment among people with autism is too high. However, compared to the eighties, the situation in Flanders has improved a lot. We now have services from early childhood to adulthood:

- Diagnostic centers connected to universities
- Specialized schools and classrooms for autistic children
- Support for autistic students in mainstream education
- Group homes
- Supportive employment programs

- Social-skills training
- Home training; we started with four home trainers in 1986 and now have around two hundred home trainers in Flanders

Services in Belgium continue to rely on the TEACCH principles. Peter's wife, Det Dekeukeleire, adds,

If Gary were to visit classes in Flanders now, he would still see his influence. While we have changed things over the years to adapt to European culture, the TEACCH principles continue to be the foundation of the services we provide for people with autism and their families.

Brazil

Viviane de Leon says,

TEACCH has had a huge impact on the understandings, treatments, and training methods in Brazil. Before 1990 there was nothing in the way of education or in schools, and autism was treated as a mental illness. When we brought TEACCH to Brazil, we emphasized the need to have a different perspective on ASD based on learning styles and to include people with ASD in schools and the therapies.

The importance of TEACCH in Brazil is immeasurable. Through many trainings and conferences, Eric and Gary didn't just give lessons; they shared experiences of life. TEACCH always works with families. Eric and Gary gave us strategies to teach parents to use at home. They are both visionaries ahead of their time.

In 2018 I organized the first workshop [on] fundamentals of TEACCH in Rio de Janeiro, when Kaia Mates and Allison

Butwinsk presented the principles founded by Gary and Eric for forty professionals and parents. In 2019 I took two groups of professionals from different states in Brazil for the five-day training in Chapel Hill so that these professionals [could] be certified to conduct TEACCH training in Brazil.

This year, 2022, two more international events are planned in Brazil with the TEACCH staff. We will share knowledge about TEACCH with approximately sixty-four professionals and enable twenty-four of them to go forward to their TEACCH certification. All this effort is to share the ideas of Gary and Eric here in Brazil with as many more families as we can. My idea is to build the culture of autism and help people with ASD have a high quality of life. I hope my dream can come true.

Canada: Ontario and Quebec

Maureen Bennie tells us,

Lots of people in Canada went to Chapel Hill for their summer training sessions. School boards would come and send some of their people. I ran conferences throughout Canada and in Southern England, and Gary spoke at several locations in Canada including Calgary, Edmonton, and Vancouver. I train trainers who then go out to different parts of Canada and other countries to train others.

Nathalie Plante says,

In 1980 we didn't know much about autism, but there were a lot of people who today would have been diagnosed. Many were in hospitals and needed a better quality of life. In 1990 I began teaching and had two students with the diagnosis of ASD. A psychologist, Gilbert Leroux, went to Chapel Hill and came back and said, "This is what we need." We requested TEACCH training, and Mary Beth brought a team in 1993. John Dougherty brought teams each of the following two years—each time in Montreal. Each year we added more of our own trainers. I was cotrainer with Eric Schopler's daughter-in-law, Janet Martin. Then we opened places throughout the province.

I was translating for twenty-five participants; most didn't speak English, and the TEACCH trainers didn't speak French. In 1996 I went to Chapel Hill with three trainers from Quebec for their five-day training sequence.

Now lots of students are on the spectrum. Among the services we provide are inclusion, special classes within regular schools, and special schools for people with ASD. We prepare students starting around age fifteen with internships for three or four years in a row so they can get hired when they are eighteen.

We have brought in many speakers from TEACCH, such as Mary Beth to talk about sexuality and Mike Chapman on employment support and Cathy Faherty to speak about her book *Asperger's and Me*. Gary was a speaker around 2009. Lee Marcus is part of the history of TEACCH, and he has been here.

TEACCH has done a lot for us in Quebec. School boards have chosen TEACCH for services. We provide a regular teacher and a specialist in every classroom, and we speak of Structured Teaching a lot. I have fifteen trainers who work with me, and we conduct five-day trainings, during which participants bring videos of their classrooms, and we offer feedback. This gets the best results. We do as much training as possible because there are many new teachers entering the profession I do two and three-day training. Two and five years ago, I conducted training in Quebec City. Soon I will be in Gatineau.

As the pandemic recedes, I want to resume sending people to Chapel Hill so I'll have people to take over if I want to slow down.

TEACCH has inspired us to design a tool to help people provide a schedule that people with ASD can use. This is a tribute to TEACCH from me because they gave us so much. It will be a good legacy of what TEACCH has done for us. It is an assessment tool that takes sixty to ninety minutes. It will be easier for professionals to use. It will first identify what the child can understand: pictures, words (verbal and/or written), objects, pictograms.

Sometimes we can show a child an empty juice box, and he might understand it is snack time. Maybe we can show the child a figurine or a book to let him understand he is about to go home. The teacher or parent must be near the child to help the child become independent more quickly. But we have to be careful with our prompting. If a child doesn't know how to do something independently, we have to be careful not to provide too much help.

Denmark

Maureen Bennie says that "Denmark is advanced with TEACCH principles."

Svany relates that

> Gary visited Denmark—Arhus and Copenhagen. I attended one of his TEACCH trainings there several years back, and he has had a great influence in Denmark.

Susanne Hvidtfeldt and Regnar Hintze Thisted are TEACCH advocates in Denmark. Susanne told me,

> In 1998 the status in Denmark was that there were a lot of good services for people with ASD, especially in special schools, but

there were battles among professionals about which were the best ways to provide services. Then our leader went to Belgium for the five-day training and presentations. A second leader joined him the second week of such training.

Afterward back in Denmark, they conferred and agreed they should consider using TEACCH principles. They liked the TEACCH approach. Too much of what we were doing was in writing and oral. They thought the TEACCH approach was very, very good. What we liked was the individualization of the TEACCH approach and the environment it created: the people with ASD didn't have to change. We could let them be as they [were].

The leaders wanted to bring the best researchers in the world to Denmark. In 1990 Gary and Kaia came here for a two-day conference. Then in 1990–91, Kathy and Gary conducted their five-day training model in Denmark. They did the five-day training, always with Gary here, until 2010. We continue to do the annual presentations, and Gary last presented in 2014.

Around 2007 Mike Chapman and John Thomas from TEACCH came and implemented the TTAP, the Supported Employment program, in Denmark. The Danish trainer group and John and Mike transformed it into Danish culture. We set up a five-day training with TTAP. The adults stayed both at the training site and in the different work locations and private business so the participants could learn how the TEACCH principles could be used in work life for people with autism.

Mike Chapman explains TTAP:

TTAP stands for the TEACCH Transition Assessment Profile. It is a manual that I authored with Schopler, Mesibov, and Thomas. It was designed to help guide professionals working in the field with autism to understand how to do effective transitioning for autistic adults. As part of that, we created a training to teach people how to use the assessment tool. The tool requires that you perform continuous, ongoing vocational and daily living skills assessments for adults. The point of TTAP is it's ongoing, and every year, you're constantly using and modifying information as students grow, learn, and develop new skills. Therefore you can go back to some of the core features of the TTAP and use it to adapt and modify existing transition or vocational plans.

Kay Shigematsu says,

In Denmark, they took people with ASD who were high on the spectrum and not with any intellectual disability, and they taught them first as a group and then integrated them into regular classes. But they first wanted to teach them to be self-advocates. They figured that people with more severe disabilities would have their own advocates. The school in Denmark was called the Sophia School.

France

Kay Shigematsu says,

In France, a parent group organized our visit, and the group organizer was the father of a child with autism living in Nice. He got connected with TEACCH, and then he and the parent group decided to fund a new school. They sent one lady, a teacher, to Chapel Hill to be trained by TEACCH. They also began a supported employment program similar to what TEACCH had started, and Dr. Sasaki wanted to see it, so we went to Nice. The parents at the school in Nice were very appreciative of the father who helped them build the new school.

Brigitte Nelles told me,

> I met Eric Schopler at a conference in Paris, and in 1986 I met
> Gary and got connected with TEACCH at a hands-on training in
> Belgium, in Antwerp, with Theo Peeters.
>
> In the 1980s the situation in France was horrible for people
> with autism and their families. We didn't even speak of adults; they
> mostly ended up with their families or in psychiatric hospitals.
> Ninety-five percent of professionals dealing with autism were psy-
> choanalysts who really believed that autism was caused by moth-
> ers who were cold and distant and that parents needed therapy
> and that they should leave their autistic child to professionals who
> knew how to cure them.
>
> I met parents of a young adolescent, Louise, in Paris. They knew
> about TEACCH, and they knew Theo Peeters in Belgium. I started
> to work with them and then did a training with Theo. At that time
> because most institutions in France were staffed by psychoanalysts,
> some parents tried to create educational programs following the
> TEACCH Model. A few parents and I, including Louise's parents,
> started an association to set up a day center for adolescents with
> autism. We started this association in 1986 in France after visiting
> the TEACCH Program in North Carolina.
>
> Our association still exists in Paris. I worked with the adoles-
> cents as a teacher but also had the role of the psychologist. From
> the early beginning, Gary supported the project. He helped us find
> a professional in North Carolina to join us, and it was Vickie Shea,
> who spent months working with me on a daily basis, trying to use
> TEACCH strategies with six adolescents.
>
> In 1992 we began annual hands-on training on the TEACCH
> approach for professionals with Gary and his colleagues. Gary came
> every year for supervision of our program and for the training. The
> five-day training is one of the most powerful training models I

have experienced. Directors would require staff members to come for the training; while some might not have chosen to come, once there, they saw the value. In Paris I had the chance to be part of the training staff in Paris and to be part of the summer training-crew program in Chapel Hill. That's where I met Susanne and Regnar from Denmark, Allison from the UK, Ken Poon from Singapore, and very dear colleagues from the United States.

Also in 1992 the association finally secured state funding covering most of its operating expenses. The program expanded in Paris: a second day center opened later in 1992, a third in 1995. Also in 2006 a full-time residential home opened in the Paris region. In France most of the innovative programs that specialized in autism were started and run by parent associations. They would get started by the parent associations and then be taken over by the state, which would provide the funding.

Very clearly the parents in France were the first to be convinced by the TEACCH approach—much more than the professionals. Parents bought in because they could see their children were happier.

Now in 2022 there are a growing number of school programs that include children in classrooms—it is a matter of law that public schools have to accept children with autism. They have a right to go to school. I have been back to Chapel Hill and TEACCH approximately fifteen times during all these years for the annual conference and to be part of the training staff for the July sessions. I did the full summer trainings (four weeks each year) as part of the crew from 2006 to 2009.

Germany

Anne Haeussler says proudly,

People say I am the one who brought TEACCH to Germany

and am responsible for it spreading throughout the country. In 1988 I joined a national parent organization because I felt that if I wanted to work in the autism field, I should be a member. I also wanted information about autism since such information was scarce.

For my thesis in 1989, I did a single case study with a young girl with autism who had severely challenging behaviors. For the individual assessment, I used the PEP (psychoeducational profile), a test that Eric and his team had designed for children who were untestable. Many autistic children were untestable because they often cannot understand and comply with the standardized instructions, and they need an individualized approach. Eric was providing alternative strategies and useful materials for testing and working with autistic children.

I had written to Eric in 1988 saying I wanted to learn about autism. He wrote back and invited me to come to Chapel Hill. I then formally applied for training with the TEACCH program. Gary also sent me letters and information once he knew I'd be coming to Chapel Hill. I graduated from university, and I came to Chapel Hill in August 1990; in 1992 I enrolled in the developmental psych program at UNC.

By 1999 I had my doctoral degree from UNC and had returned to Germany. The regional parent association asked me to design a social-skills program for a group of children and a group of adults. I modeled the groups after the social groups I had experienced in North Carolina but had to adapt them to the German context and the different organizational structure. We had a staff ratio of one to two with university students as cotrainers. This allowed for individualizing content and breaking the adult group into small groups. We presented our group methods at the National Autism Conference in 2002, and we published a book on this social-skills program in 2003 and a second book on our program in 2011. I had invited my student assistants to be coauthors.

There was no big institution behind our service, just a group of parents who were paying privately and relying on sponsors. The group for adults comprised eight participants who met for three hours every other Sunday; the children's group was designed for four children and had biweekly two-hour sessions. The long sessions were due to many participants travelling quite a distance; a shorter session would not have been time efficient.

As I began writing articles and books (ultimately ten books), people became more interested in the TEACCH program. The National Autism Society in Germany asked me to present at its annual conferences. I wrote and designed online courses. In 2005 I published *The TEACCH approach to supporting and teaching individuals with autism: Introduction to theory and practice. With a foreword by Gary Mesibov.* This book is now in its sixth printing, and its articulation of TEACCH has spread throughout the country. Gary wrote the preface. Now the principles of TEACCH are accepted practice.

I kept getting requests for information about autism and to speak to groups across the country. People also asked me to work with their children. As the number of these requests increased, I started to provide individual therapy. First, I worked out of my home. When the demand for therapy services kept growing, two colleagues, Antje Tuckermann and Markus Kiwitt, and I founded a joint business named "Team Autismus." This is an institute providing clinical services in the regional autism center.

We also offer training on the TEACCH approach. We have a comprehensive training program and provide consultation services to other institutions, such as sheltered workshops or residential programs.

Everything we do is modeled on the TEACCH program. We

still maintain a close working relationship with Mary Beth and Kathy.

I initiated a national conference for practitioners from various professional fields in Germany who apply TEACCH strategies in their support of individuals with ASD. The first German TEACCH forum was held May 12–13, 2006. The keynote speaker was Dr. Lee Marcus. The TEACCH forum has become an annual event. When funds allow, TEACCH staff [are] invited to participate as keynote speakers and for additional workshops if possible. I would love to have had Gary as a keynoter, but he was always scheduled elsewhere when I would invite him.

My aim is to provide a platform for a professional exchange of ideas with regard to the TEACCH approach and to foster networking of TEACCH-inspired people in the German-speaking world. Participants come from German-speaking countries like Austria, Switzerland, Luxemburg, Northern Italy, and Germany.

As I conversed with Anne, it occurred to me that perhaps one indicator of what Eric and Gary accomplished is that Anne and others have been able to carry the message throughout Germany without either Eric or Gary with them. I wonder how many others whom we'll never know are carrying on the TEACCH initiatives.

Greece

Vaya Papageorgiou, a child and adolescent psychiatrist, discusses her experiences starting in the 1990s, recalling that,

I had three clients with autism, and I needed to know about it. I said to myself, "I need to know, learn, and grow." There were special-education schools with autistic children. So I went to London in 1996 and studied in Birmingham at the School of Education.

In 1997 I went to Chapel Hill. Then I came back twice a year until 2010. I studied the books Eric and Gary had coauthored. In 2006 I took a job at a university. This was not a good place for me. Services related to autism were nonexistent. The government was not expressing interest in providing funding for autism, and the universities had no incentive to teach about it. I wanted to create something bigger than what I was doing, and I wanted to teach doctors.

I then transferred my efforts to working through the Autism Society of Greece and citizen groups, and I would work with people and supervise people who provide services. In 2007 we brought Gary to Greece. The way he was teaching was different from anyone else.

A most important thing I learned from TEACCH is the TEACCH philosophy; it's a framework, not just a method. I also learned to be curious and to investigate. You must find out what's going on in the minds of people with autism. And I learned how to respect the child as a person. I collaborated with everyone around me.

I also found out you can't just stay in the office; you have to get out and into the classrooms. You must be able to relate to the parents. You must know the difference between autism and other disabilities. People were always very comfortable around Gary. He was great.

Iceland

Svany says,

In 2013 I connected with Gary and asked him to come to Iceland; he lectured for two days and then visited the diagnostic center and a few classrooms. We also drove to Sólheimar Ecovillage in Iceland, where many people on the spectrum live and work.

We had lunch there and were having a conversation about their programs, and in the middle of that conversation, Gary, having noticed a person pacing the cafeteria, looked over to me and said, "Svany, you should come and stay here and help them with our strategies." This comment had an impact, because the next spring, I came to Sólheimar and volunteered for a couple of months.

This has since been my tradition—when I go to Iceland, I always spend a month or two with them and help them implement TEACCH. There are many TEACCH classrooms all over Iceland, and there are regular three-day trainings in the fundamentals of the Structured Teaching model. People from there still talk about Gary's visit.

Icelandic therapists Svany (left) and Sigrun

India

Laurie Sperry visited India between 2007 and 2013 and explains how the country's relationship to TEACCH came into being:

While working in Colorado, I was contacted by a very wealthy philanthropist, in India, who asked me to work with his son with autism. I started thinking about the idea of sustainable capacity that Gary and I frequently discussed. This philanthropist agreed that he would help me set up a school in India and pay for the building, school supplies, and staff salaries in exchange for me working with his son.

I made about fifteen trips of three weeks each to India. There was so little in India to support people with autism, or their families, so when our school was ready, there was immediately a waiting list of over three hundred people. Gary wanted to know what parts of TEACCH were most useful in an area with few resources so he could generalize that to other places with limited resources. It turns out that visual supports, schedules, work systems, and structuring tasks are a universal construct.

Gary would emphasize that resources didn't have to be fancy, didn't have to come from Kinko's or a specialty store; they could be a paper and pencil with stick-figure drawings to illustrate points to the students. "You don't need access to beautiful visuals," Gary would emphasize.

We used straw mats on the floor, using different colored mats to physically structure the environment, letting students know what activities happened and where. We used visual schedules and work systems that we drew by hand to let students know what was going to happen and when and what was expected of them. I was able to take one of my graduate students from TEACCH with me on a couple of occasions. Dr. Brian Boyd started out as a teacher's aide when he was twenty-one, and he would help me in the TEACCH preschool; he is now a well-respected academic at the University of Kansas.

Ireland

Anne McGuire worked with Steve Love at first and then others for over a decade of trips to Ireland, which is a small country. According to Anne, "Ireland is probably implementing the TEACCH principles in most of its classrooms." Anne recalls how

> Two Irishwomen shadowed us because they were then able to become trainers and then could become sought-after consultants who could follow up on what we had done. I went to Ireland two or three times a year, and each time we trained a different group of teachers. Over time they gained an appreciation that kids with IEPs weren't mean spirited or brats, but their tantrums and other outbursts were their way of communicating with us through their behaviors. Behaviors are communicative."

Steve Love adds,

> The Ireland Mental Health Board wanted us. This was in the late 1990s or early 2000s. We did a few workshops and a series of lectures. Later we did weeklong trainings of the model Gary developed. The Department of Education wanted a train-the-trainers model, so some of their teachers would copresent with us. This indicated to us that they embraced TEACCH. Lee did some of this training. We were two popular people, and we returned six or seven times.
>
> From the lectures and workshops for the Health Board, we saw changes in individual practices from those who attended. The

impact was much greater when people would attend from schools and then return to their own schools and spread the practices.

Israel

Cory Shulman says,

In the early 1980's, Lee Marcus came to Israel. He and Gary had worked together seamlessly. I was working on autism at the time and someone connected us, and that was my introduction to TEACCH. I would come to Chapel Hill where I continued to strengthen my relationship with Lee and Gary. I participated in TEACCH workshops as well as presenting some of the amazing work being done in Israel according to the TEACCH principles. Lee continued to return to Israel to present and coach until his retirement in 2008. I participated in TEACCH workshops as well as presenting some of the amazing work being done in Israel according to TEACCH principles. Lee continued to return to Israel to present and coach until his retirement in 2008.

In Israel we have so much to be thankful for to TEACCH and not just for being the first to provide resources and training of its kind but also because as TEACCH changed training and intervention delivery all over the world, it has shaped our philosophy and services in Israel.

In 1978 Israel was behind the United States in providing support services. Autism was still seen as a form of mental illness. Lee came and really did some great things, reinforcing and elaborating on what was only beginning to emerge in care for people with autism and their families. In 1980, We set up the first recognized educational program in Jerusalem with only nine professionals.

Today there are over 150 programs for students with autism reflecting a continuum of services which is fundamental to the

TEACCH principles. In addition we have over 38 stellar researchers involved in the Autism Center of the Hebrew University doing amazing research in autism. Over the years I have sent seven people to Chapel Hill to be trained by TEACCH and I'm sure others in Israel have also sent many people there. We use the TEACCH model in training both diagnostic and educational teams today.

Jordan and Qatar

Laurie Sperry worked with teachers in Jordon and Qatar in 2016 and 2017, helping them build capacity within their schools. Laurie made three trips, staying two weeks at a time.

Latvia

Maureen Bennie presented in Latvia as recently as early February 2022.

Mexico

Steve Love tells us that

In 1996–97 a family with a Japanese husband and Mexican wife contacted TEACCH, possibly Gary, and I went to Mexico twice. Catherine Faherty had been to Mexico to train, and then we both went back. I did diagnostic work; she did Structured Teaching.

Autism was not much on their radar when I was there; however, Catherine and Gary travelled there quite a bit to do training. The Mexican people we worked with had an enthusiasm for learning and asked good questions. There was an interested audience of about 150 people the first time we were there. It was a mixed audience of professionals, parents, and teachers.

Pakistan

Andy Short worked mostly part time with Eric and TEACCH, working with families who sought TEACCH evaluation and treatment from outside of North Carolina, often from other countries. Andy says, "We worked with families coming from England, France, Japan, Iraq, India, Pakistan, the Soviet Union, Singapore, United Arab Emirates; they came to work with Eric. I worked with Eric, Miggie Schopler (Eric's second wife), and others to evaluate these children and provide recommendations for treatment and consultation.

Romania

Svany says, "I went to Romania with two teachers from Iceland who were not certified as TEACCH trainers, and they needed someone to accompany them who was. We went to Romania to do three-day TEACCH trainings there for two weeks, and it became popular there and still is. The TEACCH approach is being used in Romania today in several places."

Russia

Susan Moreno tells a story about a high-ranking Russian official whose daughter was autistic. According to Susan,

> The Russian system for providing services for people with autism was in chaos in the 1900s. People with autism just disappeared from view. Gary once said he had a call from someone at the Russian embassy. This person said it must be kept quiet, but he wanted Gary to recommend treatment for the autistic daughter of this Russian cabinet member. It may have been Foreign Minister Eduard Shevardnadze; it was definitely a high-ranking official. He said the girl could come for as long as necessary, but it must be kept hush-hush.

The girl did come to Chapel Hill to be examined for the purpose of learning how to prepare her for adulthood. Her father did not come with her, and I'm not sure if the mother did. After a month Gary met with this emissary, who was obviously filling in for people at a higher level. Gary told him that because the situation had gone too long without the appropriate interventions, any improvement they could expect would be limited.

The emissary handed the report back to Gary, and as Gary and others looked on in astonishment, the emissary said, "Of course we won't give this report to him. In Russia we don't give bad news."

Saudi Arabia

Laurie Sperry has worked in Saudi Arabia, and she explains,

A family from Saudi Arabia paid for my postdoctoral work in Chapel Hill. They would fly their entourage over to Chapel Hill to TEACCH. They were bringing this family to work with Gary and me. I also made trips to Saudi Arabia. Gary told me, "Take a book with you; you will have long waits." This was sound advice. Sometimes you'd wait for hours, and then someone would say, "Can you come back tomorrow instead?" Some people would get aggravated. I would get aggravated.

The entourage they would bring to Chapel Hill might include two direct caregivers, a gentleman who arranged providers for the little boy, and two family members.

Gary would also go there to work with the family. This family funded building of a Vocational Rehabilitation Center in 1997 and named it after the prince who funded it. They always came over to see me in the United States.

In 2015 I returned to Saudi Arabia, and I helped them set up a rehabilitation site, and I did a weeklong training. TEACCH has had a pervasive influence in the country. In the fourteen years since I had previously been there, I could see Gary's impact and the impact of TEACCH. They had spent millions on their vocational rehabilitation center. I was amazed at how far they had come and the huge impact of TEACCH.

Their center was extremely well equipped. The staff were highly trained. The resources were state of the art. The tasks they were teaching the people with autism were meaningful and could result in gainful employment. All of those things reflect the values of Gary and TEACCH.

Gary once told me that it was the king of Saudi Arabia, whose grandson had autism, which led to the interest in providing services. However, in Saudi culture, a person with autism or any other disability was not valued, and therefore, according to Gary, people working on behalf of TEACCH were asked to keep the identity of the child and his grandparent hush-hush.

Singapore

Ken Poon is associate professor, Nanyang Technological University, Singapore, and president of the Rainbow Resource Center. Ken says,

> Services for people with ASD have grown quite a lot since the 1970s and '80s, when autism wasn't a word here. The Rainbow Resource Center was founded in 1987 by one of our professors and conducted its first small conference in 1989. The center provided early intervention services and services for children with severe disabilities.
>
> I have been president of a charity that supports people with ASD and their families. Our charity, the Autism Resource Center, not to be confused with the Rainbow Resource Center mentioned above, was founded by a group of parents because they wanted

training, and we held our first conference in 1999. Gary came here in the late '90s, and I first met him in 2000 when he conducted training in a large way. He then came once a year for many years.

Gary is undoubtedly one of the giants who shaped how we serve individuals with autism in Singapore. He has, over the past twenty years, inspired and trained generations of professionals serving persons with autism. I'm one of them, and I had the privilege of not only learning from him in Singapore but also benefiting from his mentorship during my years at UNC Charlotte (2002–2005) and beyond.

The program Gary brought to Singapore changed how we were doing things. He and Eric Schopler have trained thousands of our people across many generations over the years. Gary helped me move away from thinking I could tell people what to do and instead to an approach of trying to understand how people with ASD think and then building on their strengths. He always brought parents into the picture and tried to understand where people with ASD were strong and where they were weak.

On a personal level, he tried to understand that these were people with autism, not autistic people.

One reason I went to North Carolina was because it was the first state that had cradle-to-grave services. Now Singapore has changed a lot. We are now a regional hub where people come to us for services and training. We were asked by Saudi Arabia to help them establish an autism program. Gary has brought this about. Some people come to us to learn by being here, some come for courses we offer, and some come by invitation of one of our people, and this is largely because of the foundation of our work built on what we have learned from TEACCH.

I work with parents and make sure we are providing appropriate services. We not only serve children directly but also provide them a place to go. And we offer sibling programs and family support. This all definitely grew out of TEACCH. Some parents can be difficult to deal with; however, we continue to support the children even if the parents are not "polite."

Gary's sense of humor is witty and comes through his storytelling. Some people are caustic and funny; Gary's humor is never caustic or mean. He catches details and tells stories in a very respectful fashion, not at anyone's expense. My experience with Gary is that he is always very respectful, and he knows how to get things done. He spoke of the role of pets because they provide companionship, and it is difficult for people with ASD to gain companionship from people.

It makes a big difference when Gary tells you that he appreciates what you are doing. He wants to learn what we can do to improve the quality of life of people with ASD.

Mike Chapman is credited with helping Singapore set up a supported employment program that is a model for other countries. Mike relates that

In addition to sending me to Singapore for the first of my many trips there, to help set up their first Supported Employment program, Gary ended up making many trips of his own to Singapore and we trained people from there in Chapel Hill. The people in Singapore love him. If they learn of his illness, so many of them will feel so badly. The people in Singapore worship the ground he walks on. Whenever I am there, they always ask about him even if it has been a while since his last visit.

Laurie Sperry explains that

The wealthy funder of the school in India was living in Singapore, so after visiting India, I would go to Singapore. I suggested to this wealthy gentleman that he should hire two young men to hang out with his son. He hired two eighteen-year-olds, and a few years later, they founded their own company called INCLUS, which focuses on vocational education for young adults with autism. This is one example of the circle of influence Gary had.

South America, in Addition to Brazil

Susan Moreno, Indiana, says,

> Before Cathy Pratt and I handed off our conferences to the National Association of Autism, people came from all over South America. A principal in Bogota, Columbia, came with four of his teachers. Eventually Cathy and I went to Bogota and went to every country in South America to do training except Venezuela.

South Korea

Joanne Quinn began training in South Korea twenty-three years ago, and the trainees are still using it.

Spain

David Preece referred me to Joaquin Fuentes, whom he described as "the man behind GAUTENA," an autism organization in the Basque Country in Northern Spain. Joaquin was trained as a psychiatrist in Albany, New York, and as a child and adolescent psychiatrist in Pittsburgh, Pennsylvania, spending a total of four years in the United States. After finishing his training, he returned to his hometown, San Sebastián, Spain. Here is his story about the impact of TEACCH in Spain:

> TEACCH has had an impact on millions of families, and I mean millions, and indeed has had a tremendous impact in our area, a province of the Basque region of Spain.

In 1981 two professionals from our charity, GAUTENA (Gipuzkoa Autism Society), the executive director and myself, their medical advisor, attended the Autism Society of America Conference in Boston. We heard a presentation by Eric Schopler, and we became so excited when learning about the TEACCH program that we made arrangements to visit Chapel Hill immediately after the conference instead of returning to Spain. We realized that we shared the same basic philosophy and approach to autism.

The TEACCH program gave us a different perspective. Its approach said that not only are families not bad; they can help us. Prior to the findings of Eric and others, even as late as the 1980s in some places, families were thrown away. Eric, and then Gary with Eric, helped us see that we needed to train parents how to support their children.

When we heard from Eric Schopler that the TEAACH program had been mandated to serve the citizens of the state of North Carolina, we knew that this was what we needed. Eric Schopler and his wife, Margaret Lansing, Miggie, came to San Sebastian in 1985 for our first international conference on autism. Since then staff from TEACCH and from GAUTENA have participated in many autism-related international events, and this has fostered a mutually cherished relationship. Gary and Eric inspired us about the tasks ahead.

We needed to translate and adapt tests and assessment instruments, many of which we are still using across Europe today. And we integrated into our practice the many key TEACCH principles, including:

1. Autism "belongs" to the brain. We were so happy to find allies in this revolutionary way of thinking about autism (at that time).
2. Families and friends are critically important to support people with autism so they can enjoy a productive, happy life. We, the

specialists, serve as their coaches, and we do not substitute for family.

3. The diagnosis of autism informs us about the condition, but it does not tell us about the person. People with autism are so diverse that we must personalize. This individualization (knowing their limitations, strengths, and dreams) tells us how to support them.

4. We must have open, specialized classrooms in our school system. In fact, we closed years ago our small special school and migrated into the supported regular system. And in the following years, we developed day centers for adults, where they accessed supported employment, group homes, respite care, supported leisure, and so forth. We pursue a fully inclusive society.

5. In order to support people with autism and their families, you should not literally copy a program. You must understand your local values, culture, and resources and adapt. We do not have formal training initiatives like those in North Carolina, but we receive visits and have exchanged staff and families, mainly via Autism Europe.

We learned these principles of TEACCH and then adapted them to our county when we returned to Spain after my first visit to Chapel Hill:

1. We explained to parents that we needed them, and a parent society was glad to offer its support.

2. Our staff had to be trained to use diagnostic tests.

3. We opened units in schools consisting of five children with autism, and for each unit there would be a teacher, an aide, and two family members. Where possible there would be inclusion in regular classes.

4. Children in regular classes would volunteer at times to be special tutors, and this would change the entire atmosphere in a school.

TEACCH has trained people from all over the world. I have delivered conferences in more than thirty countries on all continents and always found people who had been informed about TEACCH and to whom I could reinforce with our practice. I remember quite well sharing conferences with Gary in France, where the autism field is still undeveloped and influenced by psychological theories. I remember that Eric and I dared to give a speech together at La Sorbonne campus in Paris. French families were thrilled!

Our program received the European Citizen Award in 2016 from the European Parliament. According to the jury, we had put into practice in our GAUTENA program the support for citizens with ASD under the values that define and should characterize Europe. This has been the only time that a program for ASD has achieved this high international recognition.

We can't cure autism. However, TEACCH has the ingredients to change the quality of life. We must, therefore, recognize the TEACCH program for what they have done. People like Eric Schopler and Gary Mesibov and many other North Carolina team members have been fundamental for us. We are so happy to recognize our heritage and feel proud of sharing their inspiring model. They have changed the lives of all of us.

Well done, Gary. ¡ Muchas gracias!

Sweden

Anne McGuire did TEACCH training in Sweden:

After three years of occasional work in Sweden, I felt the teachers understood the thinking behind the methodology. In Sweden they have a culture of compassion, and they work as a community to support the elderly, so TEACCH principles are compatible with their nature.

Steve Love says,

> In Sweden they had the broadest embrace of Structured Teaching. Our training was sponsored by their Autism Society, and they were using many models but embraced ours. We had different people doing preschool, elementary, adolescent, and adult. Maybe five or six of their people trained with us so they could be trainers when we were no longer there. Mary Beth and I did a residential model. People from group homes came. We focused on how to bring Structured Teaching into their environment.

Svany adds,

> I did a few lectures in Sweden, and TEACCH is very popular there.

Birgitta Karlsson, who lives and does TEACCH training in Sweden, recalls,

> In 1999 we had two group homes and eight people. I went to a five-day TEACCH training session, and at that time, I was working with eight clients, each of whom had autism and intellectual disabilities. Initially following the training, we just copied what we had been taught. We were taught that everyone with autism should have a picture schedule.
>
> This worked with two of the eight clients but not as well with the other six because they were at different levels of understanding. In 2001 we contracted with someone who brought in TEACCH training through the Central Concrete Communications Company from Belgium. Mary Beth Van Bourgondien of TEACCH came as a supervisor for the Swedish team that conducted the training.
>
> There is a huge difference between how autism was viewed

years ago and now and also the amount of training. Then, you had to be in the frame; never go outside the frame. Inflexible. Every day should be the same. For example, if you went for pizza every Saturday, you did not go on a Tuesday one week to change the routine. We have learned to train our clients to be more flexible. Therefore, clients are not as sensitive to change now as they were twenty-three years ago.

Here is an example of a step-at-a-time process for helping clients to be more flexible: In the morning, if their routine is to make the bed, go to the bathroom, then shower, you might change it by changing one thing: bathroom, shower, make bed. Just one change in the schedule. Small steps.

One activity we would do with people with ASD would be to sort cards into different containers by categories.

In 1999 everyone was blaming the parents. Mothers weren't giving enough love. Parents weren't strict enough. One client, when he moved here in 2005, had been in group homes because his parents couldn't cope with him and the belief that his autism was caused by the mother. This is the longest he's been in any home—since 2005, sixteen years.

Mary Beth Van Bourgondien visited our place at Sjöarp group homes three times—2012, 2013, and 2014. Gary and TEACCH have quite a big status here in Sweden because of their impact on autism research and services. The principles of TEACCH have spread through Sweden over the years.

In Sweden today diagnoses of autism are increasing in children and young people. I think this is partly because knowledge among both professionals and parents has increased, but a large part, at least in Sweden, is due to the school methods being changed ten years ago. Before it was changed, the teacher taught a lot on the blackboard for the whole class and told the students what work to do. Today students from a very early age must take responsibility for their own learning, This becomes difficult for people on the autism spectrum, who have difficulty planning and seeing the whole picture.

Brigitte offers these anecdotes:,

I have a stepson, eight years old, with high functioning autism. There is a sausage that comes in two sizes. The name of the big sausage is Bullens hot dog, and the smaller sausage, Bullens Lager hot dog. My son had always had the smaller sausage, and it fit perfectly on the bun he would have with it. He went to a party where they served the larger of the two sized sausages. He wouldn't eat it because it extended beyond the outer edges of the bun, and he needed it to be the same size.

Also, my son is very particular about foods. The meat has to be on the left side of the plate, the potatoes on the right side, for example. He is not comfortable going to school if his jacket is cold. It has to be warmed up.

One of our clients was shopping in the store with members of our staff. He had unpacked his goods for payment. This client always used to go and sit on a chair that was at the exit of the store to wait for the staff to pay before it was time to pack down the goods. On this day, an elderly man was sitting on the chair when our client was on his way there. A staff member asked him where he was going, and he replied, "I'm moving the older man." In his world the chair was his, regardless of whether someone else was sitting on it or not. He does not have the ability to generalize knowledge.

Switzerland

Brigitte Nelles says,

> I met Cecile Coudert, a young psychologist, when I moved to the Eastern part of France, near Switzerland. I live close to the Swiss border, and since 2006, I work half time in France and half in the French-speaking part of Switzerland.
>
> In 2006 the French-speaking part of Switzerland, in regard to autism, was not very different from the French situation in the 1990s. Similar to France, the psychoanalytic influence is strong. In this part of Switzerland, parents also have to fight for the right of their children to go to school.
>
> It is surprising in a country that is progressive in so many ways that it is behind the times with support for people with autism and their families. It is different in German-speaking parts of the country, where it is much more usual for children with autism to go to regular schools.
>
> My work is primarily training professionals and parents. I go to schools and to group homes, where I work with professionals to support them. More and more, people are getting trained in educational approaches, and TEACCH principles and strategies are very commonly known, but not always well enough to implement them.

Part Three: States in the United States

Alaska

Tom Schopler says, "Gary took trainers to Alaska, and they worked at two schools where they do TEACCH training."

Arizona

Svany says,

In 1996 I moved back to the [United States] to Arizona from Iceland. Few in Arizona had heard of autism or TEACCH. I started volunteering in the schools in Scottsdale. The director of the special-education programs in Scottsdale, Joanne Phillips, had a meeting with me to ask where I had gotten my knowledge, and I said it was from TEACCH.

She was so impressed with the results of setting up visual supports in the classrooms that she asked me to get in touch with the people in North Carolina and ask them to come and train our teachers here in Scottsdale. In Arizona Joanne and I have probably been the strongest voices for TEACCH.

Joanne Phillips was in the Deer Valley Unified School District from 1985 to 1991, and she relates that

I started the first dedicated public school autism program using nonverbal and visual supports. In 1975 the Education for All Handicapped Children Act had just been enacted, entitling special-education students the right to an appropriate education. At that time services for kids with autism were nonexistent in public schools. Most public school educators had never even heard of autism.

In 1991 I became the district director of special education in the Scottsdale Unified School District and, again, began the task of creating district programs and interventions that were more appropriate and inclusive. Staff training was a needed priority. In 1994 there were still no quality autism services in the state because there weren't any trained staff in autism strategies. The universities were not providing training in autism, there was no teacher certification in autism, and many school psychologists were not trained in evaluating students with autism. That's when I met Svany; we talked in my office for a few hours, and we just clicked.

Svany talked to Gary, requesting that TEACCH trainers conduct a five-day training in Arizona, and Gary sent a TEACCH training team that included Jack Wall and Svany. I observed the training and was blown away. I had parents telling me, "I heard my child speak for the first time. We actually talked together!"

I made sure to have all of my teachers who were showing an interest [in] and understanding of autism and who actually liked these kids participate in the first training. That's how we started: with a strong trained staff. We brought the TEACCH trainers out twice a year for seven years.

We partnered with TEACCH to redesign our trainings, and we reduced the training from five days to three days; we used videotapes of students of all ages and degrees of autism. This overcame the problem of a parent calling the day their child was to participate and saying he'd had a meltdown and couldn't come. We built up a library of videos of students in various contexts, obtaining parent permission to film children to use in the trainings. Parents were more than willing to have their kids be a part of this amazing training.

In 2003–2007 I became Arizona's state director of special education and used the opportunity to make a statewide impact. I started an autism initiative with Svany as the coordinator. We brought in experts from all over the country for autism-focused conferences and training. This is when Gary first came to Arizona himself, spending two days with our district teams. I knew what was needed firsthand as a local director. I funded statewide training cohorts with each district, sending a team to learn and bring back what they were learning to their districts to train their staffs. Training became more powerful as coaching of teams continued.

As state director I wore two autism hats. One was continuing the TEACCH training, sponsored by my professional organization, in which I became the facilitator. The other was adding a new set of team cohorts annually, with Gary returning to Arizona to prepare each new cohort.

I retired from the Arizona State Department of Education in 2007, opening my own consulting firm. I then took full control of the TEACCH trainings, maintaining a close relationship with TEACCH Chapel Hill and Gary. We developed a two-day advanced training model, going into more depth, with Gary as the trainer. He was amazing! He so easily translated strategies across age and functioning levels, making it seem like such common sense. I don't think I have ever seen high school teachers [as] engaged as when he spoke about transition services and how to identify transition IEP [Individual Education Plan] goals, clearly linking them to community settings and the workplace and postgraduation, rest-of-your-life reality.

Svany says,

I have fifteen grandchildren, and four have autism. There is so much more to do. I just finished a four-day TEACCH training for Navajo country two weeks ago and then did a follow-up visit to Kayenta [Unified] School District for five days. This was a visit to support implementation of TEACCH principles. Poverty in Navajo country is horrible. One-third of the people do not have running water. Every year we do TEACCH training there in July, August, and September.

In 1996 when I returned to the United States from Iceland, there was nothing for people with autism. Now there are lots of schools, and TEACCH has had a significant impact on services for people with autism and their families. They love the TEACCH approach.

Colorado

Laurie Sperry says,

> For six years I worked as a principal investigator with the Professional
> Development in Autism Center in Colorado, which focused in part
> on establishing TEACCH programs throughout the United States,
> including Kansas, South Dakota, and Minnesota, as well as Colorado.

Hawaii

Laurie Sperry cites a 1994 federal consent decree in which the judge ordered the state of Hawaii to hire five experts in education and mental
health in the autism field to restructure services for people with disabilities
in the state:

> I was hired right out of my postgraduate program as the state direc-
> tor of autism services. Gary quipped that I was the only graduate
> student who ever quadrupled her salary upon graduation.
>
> I used the same concept that was used to set up the TEACCH
> centers throughout North Carolina: a hub-and-spoke model. I set
> up regional centers within school districts throughout the state of
> Hawaii. Teachers would come to the centers for internships, just
> as they used to come to our summer TEACCH trainings. Then
> they would go back to their classrooms and set up a program there.
> Gary and I talked a lot about building sustainable capacity. This
> was also how TEACCH spread through the United States.
>
> While in Hawaii I ran into a person who had come to a
> TEACCH training at Chapel Hill and asked if I would go to
> Saipan. I went twice and took two colleagues and set up two sites
> there; I went for three weeks each time. The idea was always to
> build capacity within local communities using the resources that
> were available.

Indiana

Cathy Pratt says,

There was some intensifying of the influence of TEACCH and Gary's legacy in Indiana when we were selected to be part of the National Professional Development Center on Autism Spectrum Disorder (NPDC) grant in 2011 (autismpdc.fpg.unc.edu). Each of the educational consultants at my office was attached to a school site to support them in implementing EBPs (evidence-based practices) for students with autism. Some of the EBPs were components of Structured Teaching, and we were using detailed fidelity checklists devised by NPDC to support schools in implementation.

Once the grant was over, the work was so successful that my office continued to offer similar levels of support to more schools, spreading the knowledge even further.

Toni Flowers adds,

In 1975 Indiana started a pilot program for people with typical autism—noncommunicative and/or behavioral problems. When I saw these people, I just got hooked. However, in the 1970s no one knew much about autism or what to do. Our first director had a PhD in sign language, so we started with that. We did nothing sensory, nothing to do with addressing behaviors. Now we and parents have learned so much.

As I learned how sensory issues could affect all five senses or any combination, I was able to look at my students with a fresh eye. I realized that if what came in through the sense was distorted, then a person's reaction to such stimuli would also be distorted. It was another awakening moment for me.

In the early nineties, I went to Chapel Hill for the five-day training, and it all came together. It just changed everything. I returned to Indiana, and the light bulb had gone off. I immediately put up schedules, used paper clips (no Velcro in those days), and I utilized workstations and visuals as I had learned in Chapel Hill. From then until COVID, I would go into classrooms and demonstrate working with people with ASD.

The principles of TEACCH have been accepted in Indiana. At first it was viewed as too much work, but now we have seen the results and have learned that if you take the time, it becomes much easier for the people with autism and the people supporting them. There is admittedly a lot of up-front work required. Gary visited our intensive program a while back, and of course I had been to Chapel Hill. Gary and TEACCH have had such a profound effect on what I do.

Catherine Davies says,

One of my colleagues, Amy Gaffney, has also become trained by TEACCH, and she and I have both become TEACCH certified advanced consultants under the certification program that TEACCH introduced, I think, around 2013. So now both of us are using Structured Teaching to inform our work across Indiana.

Iowa

Kelly Trier recalls her experiences in Iowa:

In my search for effective ways to support people with autism, I found TEACCH strategies in around the late 1980s/early 1990s. I became an autism consultant part time and continued my work as an SLP in a Southern, rural, poverty-stricken part of Iowa.

There was no training in the part of Iowa where I worked in 1987. Any training required searching for it or going somewhere else and bringing what you learned back to train others. I continued learning and taking as much training as I could so that I could train others to learn.

The TEACCH strategies were amazing in what they did for the students, and they did not require a big budget to put them in place. TEACCH strategies were my go-to for helping hundreds of kids and hundreds of staff people that I helped train in Iowa.

The visual structures of TEACCH have made a huge impact on my life and the lives of thousands in my state. These strategies reduce stress and anxiety and provide predictability in an unpredictable world; they focus on teaching independence and help individuals with ASD to understand the world around them. The strategies of TEACCH gave me a core base for helping others and a starting place for helping others when there were no other resources available.

New York

Before settling in Arizona, Joanne Phillips had been raised on Long Island, New York, and went on a full scholarship to Hofstra to become a speech pathologist:

In 1975 the professor who was my mentor told me he had a clinical practicum at Maimonides, a private school [that] was, in essence, a dumping ground for children with severe disabilities who had been expelled from their school districts due to being uncontrollable, usually having severe behavioral disturbances, including children with autism. We were to evaluate all three hundred children. If they were violent, they were being classified as emotionally disturbed. If they had bizarre behaviors and were verbal, they were [classified] as schizophrenic. If they had bizarre behaviors and were nonverbal, they were autistic. Of course, as we applied a clinical diagnosis, they hardly had any rights.

Anne McGuire says,

> When I first worked in Westchester, there was very little use of Structured Teaching and very little awareness of it. The administrator who was our liaison really helped teachers to adapt to TEACCH philosophy and use visuals in their classrooms. Over time there was a greatly increased use of structure in the BOCES (Board of Cooperative Education Services) classrooms. I now see people with autism with whom I worked years ago working in Harris Teeter or other stores around town.

Ohio

Sloane Burgess has done TEACCH training in North Carolina, Oregon, and Pennsylvania, including in the city of Pittsburgh. She says,

> I got my master's in social work in Chapel Hill, where I did an internship. I was always interested in the different behaviors and ways of thinking of people. I worked at a group home where one person had autism. I was fascinated by him because he would cuddle or he would spell responses instead of using words, and he would keep repeating the same spellings over and over.
>
> TEACCH was a great match for me. Focusing on seeing the world through the eyes of someone with autism, I learned all kinds of strategies by seeing them through their cultural eyes. I was in Asheville working for TEACCH from 1991–2001 before moving to Ohio. People from all over the world came to North Carolina to be trained by TEACCH. We would have teams go to Chapel Hill from Ohio. The Autism Society had a summer camp, and that's

where I met Jeff. He was always super funny. At a restaurant he returned to our table after a visit to the restroom and announced, "As General MacArthur once said, 'I have returned.'"

I could count on Jeff to be boisterous, confident, and in your face. Once when he drove, he talked to himself, and I was terrified: "Well, Jeff," he would ask himself, "How do you get out of the parking lot?" Then he would answer: "The same way you got in."

As I listened to Sloane tell this story about Jeff, I thought to myself, "That could have been me." I do occasionally talk to myself like that. Maybe I don't do it to the extreme as someone with ASD might, but we should all be able to relate to people with ASD because we do exhibit some of the same behaviors, albeit not obsessively.

Steve Love told me,

We developed a strong team of teachers, and we worked with Sloan Burgess. She sent three or four people from Ohio to Chapel Hill to learn the model so they could conduct workshops back home.

Rhode Island

Joanne Quinn relates,

I went to Chapel Hill for training in 1999 for the first time and then would go there once or twice a year for additional training or to assist with the training. We would come back to Rhode Island completely enthusiastic, revitalized. I was impressed with the respect with which Gary treated the ASD people as well as the respect he gave everyone. His patience was incredible. He nursed everyone along for the full week.

Our training began twenty-three years ago, and we are still

using it. We have also worked with trainees in at least four other countries. In Rhode Island we always sent at least two people a year to Chapel Hill.

We have two demonstration classes—one in Warwick and one in East Greenwich. Over the past twenty years, we have probably reached 2,400 educators and two hundred parents a year. In 2008 we partnered with the Gateway Clinic. I think they've learned a lot from us. They asked us to go into a situation where two adults required around-the-clock supervision to control their behavior. We started to give these adults choices, and pretty soon, they didn't require twenty-four-hour supervision. One was then returned to regular classrooms (the other wasn't because of health issues).

We are concerned about increasing adult programs and just wetting our feet on that. We are working to provide a lot more services for young adults once they reach twenty-two. Until then they are entitled to services; after that they have to prove they need the services, and the government doesn't make it easy.

The TAP organization [that] I developed grew from a grass-roots group of educational professionals working to learn how to best educate students with autism in the public schools in RI. The parent voice was always of equal importance in the development of the organization. Today TAP provides training to over three thousand professionals across the globe. All of our work is based on the principles of TEACCH and Structured Teaching. We provide social-skills groups and a summer camp for 250 children, teens, and young adults. We are also the leading family support and resource center in our state.

I am passionate about informing other parents, teachers, and community members about the power and impact of TEACCH philosophies and strategies because of the impact on my son and our family.

Lore Gray says that Joanne's son, Patrick, came to school with a diagnosis, and she explains,

> I just worked from that. Generally when someone would come to me without a diagnosis, it would mean they sent them to me because they couldn't handle them due to behaviors or didn't like them because of terrible behavior or not getting along with other children. Back then teachers didn't want students with ASD. I was Patrick's teacher in kindergarten and grades one, two, three, and four.
>
> I first saw Gary present at a conference in Harrisburg, Pennsylvania. Then I harassed him with telephone calls and constantly called him seeking advice. He was always patient and helpful. Along with a few other concerned educators, we formed an organization which we called the Autism Project, but we needed Gary's guidance on how we should proceed, what we should do, how we could be effective. Without Gary's blessing all the other ducks wouldn't have lined up for us.

Wisconsin

When Jennifer Townsend moved to Wisconsin in 2009 she quickly discovered there were limited statewide supports in place for public K-12 schools; mainly insurance or private pay service was offered and that support for payment typically expired in early elementary school years.

> There was an autism society and some support groups but it appeared to be mostly amateur yet passionate efforts. With the support of an amazing director who went on to be the assistant statewide superintendent for special education and learning support services, they developed an autism specialist position at one of the state's 12 regional locations and began providing consultative services to

support individuals with autism in their neighborhood schools using TEACCH principals for their educational programming.

After two years the team grew hiring additional consultants locally and in the following years other regions began to have their own autism specialists, no longer an add-on to another position rather a full time role. At around the same time I recognized that some kids needed respite from their schools. So, I wrote a proposal for a short term program, *Distinguished Scholars Academy*, where learners with autism could go for a short period of time (not to exceed 1.5 school years) and learn how to use evidence based practices; educators could come to observe to "see it live" with their actual learners; the staff and students that supported this to happen we're outstanding humans.

In 2014 we developed state level autism mini grants for districts to use towards the implementation of evidence based practices to support learners with autism.

In 2016 we created statewide learning modules to support educators to understand autism; and we partnered with communities to promote educational opportunities for families and community members. We then did trainings with local law enforcement as well as transportation providers. Services and supports for autism were flourishing.

We continue to collaborate with what were once only private based agencies and therapists to bridge the gap between therapy and schools. Creating programming that is supportive of TEACCH principles is now the norm. We now have a statewide neurodiversity consultant to support these efforts and we offer ongoing conferences that invite families, educators and community members to participate.

Next year (2023) I will be offering a caregiver retreat (modeled after Barry Prizant's parent retreat) for people to come together and make connections with others who have been there, are there, or are headed there and wish to share their story in hopes that it will support others. The goal is to create an authentic sense of belonging for everyone where there are not experts, rather partners in the journey.

Wyoming

Steve Love led the three and five-day training in six or seven cities in Wyoming. Steve says,

Diane Edwards, a developmental pediatrician, invited us and organized the training schedule. She wanted to build a strong team that would include a speech therapist, an occupational therapist, and teachers. She brought us in many times.

Chapter Thirteen

Autism and the Criminal Justice System

People with ASD can commit legal offenses due to lack of understanding as opposed to intent, but how can they be prepared to interact in a world which they don't understand? There are no easy answers.

Kara Hume

I had spoken at length with nearly eighty people, I had outlined what I thought would be all the chapters for this book, and I had written a first draft of each chapter. All that was left, I thought, was to polish up the chapters and prepare for publication. Then someone suggested I speak with Yale University Professor Alex "Lexy" Westphal about Gary's interest in the criminal justice system and how it affects people with autism.

I knew Gary had occasionally been an expert witness at trials, but I was unaware that his interest in the criminal justice system went any further. This was another aspect of his career we had never discussed, but it was worth exploring, so I zoomed with Lexy. This led to interviews with several more people, including a follow-up interview with Laurie Sperry, with whom I had spoken at length but on topics related to many of her vast experiences with autism, not her history with autism and the criminal justice system Ultimately I spoke with

- Larry Dubin, an attorney and law professor at the University of Detroit Mercy Law School, whose son, diagnosed with autism at age twenty-seven, was arrested for having illegal sexual images on his computer (a noncontact offense) and got entangled in the legal system for more than ten years,
- Dennis Debbaudt, who has produced over forty autism-and-law-enforcement-related books, reports, and training videos since the 1990s,
- Melissa Sreckovic, associate professor of education at University of Michigan–Flint, who has delivered training courses for police officers on working with people with autism,
- Laurie Sperry, a board-certified behavior analyst and director of autism services and programs in Arvada, Colorado, who has traveled to many parts of the world as a TEACCH trainer and as an expert on autism and criminal justice,
- Kara Hume, a TEACCH trainer and associate professor at UNC, and Alexander Westphal, a forensic psychiatrist, and Yale professor specializing in autism spectrum disorder.

Gary was focused on two aspects of autism and how it is addressed in the criminal justice system:

1. to what degree the limited ability of people with autism to communicate effectively should be taken into account in their arrest and sentencing, and
2. what preventative strategies could help people with autism avoid getting caught up in the criminal justice system, such as police training and preparation programs for educating people with autism about how to act in the real world once they begin

the transition from the public education system to functioning independently as an adult in society.

People with autism are particularly susceptible to accusations of child pornography because often they learn about their own sexuality by surfing the internet rather than from direct contact with others. As Dennis explained,

> Most of us learn about our sexuality from our peer group or siblings, not our parents. In fact, when I conduct workshops and ask people, "How many of you learned about sex from your dad?" maybe one in a thousand men raise their hands. You learn from your peer groups, but you don't have much of a peer group if you are ASD and you don't go to parties and hang around with peers.

Larry Dubin explains,

> Since people with autism usually do not socialize, they spend an above-average amount of time on their computers. People with autism are tied to their computers because they find it difficult to interact with people. But they don't understand the workings of computers, so they don't understand how images can go from one computer to another and how law enforcement can find out when child pornography is being accessed. They will assume if images are freely available on their computer, it must be lawful to view them.

I had begun my exploration of autism and the criminal justice system by contacting Lexy, who related how he and Gary became acquainted. He told me,

> I knew Gary by reputation as early as 2005; however, we had never met, nor spoken with each other. In 2010 I was working with a couple of people facing ten- to twenty-year sentences

for noncontact offenses because they really didn't understand the ramifications of their actions. Around that time pediatrician Phil O'Donnell, Laurie Sperry, and I submitted a proposal for a presentation at a 2012 criminal justice conference. Laurie, who first connected with TEACCH in the early 1990s, suggested that we invite Gary Mesibov to be on our panel. "Why would someone of his stature want to be part of our presentation?" we wondered.

Gary accepted the invitation. That was the beginning of a series of email exchanges over the years whenever Gary would be involved in a situation involving a person with autism and the justice system or if he simply had a question.

Gary's interest in criminal justice was trying to understand how to support people with ASD who might violate laws unintentionally because some of the people with whom he worked would get in trouble. He approached this from a position of advocacy. He would speak of dispositions; people with ASD had no disposition to commit a crime. They might get in trouble because of their social disabilities—not recognizing social norms. For instance, they might be accused of stalking because of not being aware of the consequences of following someone and not understanding the meaning of "Leave me alone."

Or their penchant for repetition, as in the case of Darrius McCollum, which drew nationwide publicity as well as Gary's interest, might get them in trouble. The McCallum case was the basis for the 2016 documentary *Off the Rails*. According to Wikipedia McCollum was arrested more than twenty times for posing as a New York City subway motorman and bus driver and operating subway trains and buses for joyrides. According to his mother, he had been fascinated with buses and trains since his childhood and has been diagnosed with autism. Ironically, he never had an accident while illegally driving a transit vehicle.

People who had driven with him called Darius "the best driver we ever had."

Gary was acutely concerned because of a couple of what he called "ugly cases" such as McCollum's. He was interested in distinguishing between outcome-based and intent-based assessments. At the core of the problem is an inability to get good diagnoses.

Laurie Sperry echoed Lexy and told me that

One of the challenges is that the way autism is diagnosed is so different around the world. There may be many people with autism incarcerated that we don't even know about because it is so difficult to get statistics on the number of people with autism in jail relative to the general population. The Reid technique of interrogation could lead to false confessions by people with autism. For instance, how would an autistic person react to the statement, "This could go a lot more quickly if you'd just confess"?

Gary never blamed the police for unfortunate situations encountered by people with autism. One of his thoughts on this, which he might have pursued if he could have remained active a bit longer, was to develop training strands for police so they could have a better understanding of autism. Gary would often talk about the characteristics of autism and life circumstances that could put people with autism at risk. According to Laurie he was particularly interested in arson since some people with autism could be fascinated by fire without understanding its dangers.

Lexy added,

Problems encountered by people with autism when dealing with the criminal justice system often occurred in young people transitioning from home to independent living.

Laurie said that Gary would ask,

> What can we do to educate them so they will not get arrested? Gary had no answers, but he understood that there have to be consequences when anyone breaks the law. However, he was frustrated knowing that often a person with autism had no intent to break the law, as illustrated in the extreme by the McCollum case."

According to Dennis,

> Because most people on the spectrum do not have strong auditory skills and have limited social skills, it makes them susceptible to misunderstandings when confronted by the police. As an example, a police officer might ask a person with ASD, "When did you turn fifteen?" and the response might be "On my birthday." I would ask police colleagues, "If you got this answer, what would you think?" Of course they would think, "This is a smart-ass."
>
> Standard police tactics often are frightening to people with ASD or lead to misunderstandings—tactics such as getting in the face of a suspect, putting a spit hood over the face of a suspect to prevent them from biting or spitting, or telling someone they can go home if they just say what the police want to hear.
>
> How police handle a first encounter with someone with autism is critical since most mistakes arise in the immediate reaction phase. That's when violence may occur.

As I learned about Gary's interest in autism as it relates to the criminal justice system, I was reminded of something about Gary that none of his colleagues knew: the topic of a thesis he wrote in the 1970s. Gary emphasized that the consequences of someone's actions are often based on the outcome, not the intent. He and I had several times discussed that if two people each shot a person with the intent of killing them, and one victim died while the other survived, the person whose victim died would face a much more severe penalty than the person whose victim survived. Yet they both intended their victim to die, and it was pure chance that one lived and the other died. Gary's early interest demonstrated by his thesis obviously carried over to his work in autism.

Lexy told me,

> In my opinion, it was to Gary's credit that he wanted to learn and do more about the circumstances involving people with autism and the criminal justice system. Many important people have turned their backs on this problem either because of the risk involved for their reputation since this is such a controversial topic or, for good reason, not wanting to cast aspersions on people with autism. Gary's attitude was, 'This is the situation, and I want to help.'"

Larry Dubin echoes Lexy, pointing out that organizations don't do what Gary does because they don't want to give autism a bad name. Dennis agrees with Lexy's contention that important people often shy away from cases involving people with ASD:

> The problem is that when you bring attention to a case, it leaves a bad taste in the mouths of other people who feel that "I don't want these people living next door to me." This is a real problem. If you make the argument that there are special circumstances that cause a person with autism to commit a crime, at least point out that these are exceptions. Ninety nine percent of the population of autism doesn't get involved in stalking or accusations of child pornography; they figure out the difference between right or wrong.

Lexy adds,

> Gary has a pure interest in the education of children with autism. He wants justice throughout the world, and he wants people treated fairly.

Dennis Debbaudt (right) in conversation with a police commander

Larry Dubin's son Nick, who is autistic, holds a bachelor's degree in communications from Oakland University, a master's degree in learning disabilities from the University of Detroit Mercy, and a specialist degree in psychology and PsyD from the Michigan School of Professional Psychology. He has authored many books on autism spectrum disorder, including *Asperger Syndrome and Anxiety*. Nick diagnosed himself as autistic when he was twenty-seven years old as a result of taking tests while applying to register for his doctoral degree. Larry described to me the twenty-eight-month battle they had with the legal system:[4]

> I had been a law professor for forty-five years, my particular interests being legal ethics and litigation, when my son was arrested on charges of child pornography. I was well known in the local community because I would be called by the media whenever there was a case involving the criminal justice system. My son's arrest turned

---

[4] Nick Dubin has written about his experiences with the criminal justice system in *The Autism Spectrum, Sexuality, and the Law*, which includes chapters written by each of his parents. He has also written five other books about autism.

our world around. There was the potential for a ten-year prison sentence.

What was frightening was that Nick had almost quit college because he couldn't handle life in a dormitory. How could he last a day in prison? I had only been able to get him to remain in college by offering to take him to Los Angeles to be in the audience for the *Price is Right*, his favorite show. He would jump up and down as contestants were answering questions. We did in fact make that trip. By coincidence Nick was chosen from the audience, went on stage with Bob Barker, and won $6,000, which he subsequently spent on jazz recordings for his college radio program.

During Nick's battle with the criminal justice system, it was clearly established that he had no criminal intent in surfing the internet for images of sexual behavior. Nick's lawyers strongly believed and fought for him to be placed on diversion, which in Nick's situation meant [being] under court supervision for eighteen months, and then the case would be dismissed, leaving him without any criminal record. All five of the experts who evaluated Nick saw his as a special case lacking the intent to commit a crime. One of the experts hired by the prosecution was a neuropsychologist employed by the FBI who spent a day with Nick, and it was his opinion that it was appropriate for Nick to be placed in a diversion program.

The prosecution would not accept the opinion of the government's own expert and instead offered a plea agreement of five years on probation, which was ultimately reduced to three and a half years with no prison and, by law, required Nick to register as a sex offender, which all five of the experts opined was unnecessary. At the time of this writing, Nick had been on the registry for almost ten years and would, hopefully, be removed from it in the near future. People with autism want to follow rules. But it is hard for people with autism to learn the rules.

Dennis suggests that when he asks parents to "tell me the level of sexual understanding your son had as you sent him out into the world," they would ultimately describe an emotional level of a twelve-year-old child.

So what can be done and what is being done with regard to people with ASD and the criminal justice system? Dennis says,

> There are now a growing number of attorneys who specialize in the defense of people with autism. Judge Kim Taylor in North Carolina, now retired from the bench, has become a reference person for information about dealing with this subject. You can google her name and learn about her efforts.
>
> In 2008 with the support of a legislative committee including Judge Taylor, I was authorized to produce a video designed to educate police and the public about addressing the needs of people with ASD in the criminal justice system. The legislators told us, "Don't get involved in opinions of right and wrong. We want you to focus on communications and social cues—how to assess if someone is interested or understanding." What colored and shaped the whole video was more than an hour with Gary, which became the basis of an article by Judge Taylor, Gary, and me that was published in 2009.
>
> We ended the video with a scenario where someone is interrogated. We focused on the downloading and distribution of children's pornography. We staged a production of what a courtroom situation would be like. This helped to make up a series of articles that were published in the *North Carolina Law Review*.
>
> We need to start educating ASD kids when they are seven or eight on how to properly express their sexuality. They will need it by the time they are twelve. Can a person with ASD know something is a crime and yet commit it anyway? Yes. Can there be mitigating circumstances, and can you be taught otherwise? Yes.
>
> If a witness or suspect only speaks a foreign language, the law

requires that you must bring in an interpreter. We should do the same for someone with ASD—someone to interpret questions and responses. For instance, when asked a question, people with ASD often feel they are obligated to answer. They are not aware of their right to say, "I don't know," even if they don't know. As an example, a male was asked by an attorney trying to prove a point if he was pregnant, and he responded, "Yes."

There is a Florida law, the Wes Kleinert Act, which entitles people with ASD to representation. As far as I know, it's never been used. However, in the UK it's customary that as soon as the police learn a suspect is ASD, they stop everything and bring in a professional with experience in autism. There is technology that can potentially be used to send out a signal to police if there is anyone within one hundred yards who is ASD.

Melissa Sreckovic was a doctoral student in Chapel Hill in 2012 with an office across the hall from Gary's. Melissa recalls,

Gary gave me Nick Dubin's book on bullying and asked me to read it and give him feedback. Then he explained Nick's case. At the time Gary was advocating for diversionary alternatives to criminal convictions.

Gary was a speaker at a conference at Oakland University in Michigan, and he and I have stayed in touch. My efforts to improve situations involving people with ASD and the criminal justice system include having reached out to the local police chief and asking, "Would you like training for your police officers?" Since then I have worked with the Law Enforcement Officers Regional Training Commission in Flint, Michigan, which serves sixty agencies.

Officers have loved the training. They are very curious and ask lots of questions. I tell them when they want advice, "We are here to help." Also, we hosted Officer Friendly Day this past April at the University of Michigan–Flint. We offered lots of activities, a fun day, and a chance for people with ASD to speak with officers or listen to them read stories. Next year we will offer a simulated traffic stop so autistic individuals can practice what to do if they get pulled over.

There was a recent episode where an ASD person didn't move quickly enough for officers as he exited from his car and searched for his identification card, and the situation escalated. Creating opportunities for autistic individuals to learn and practice what to do when pulled over can help create safer interactions during a traffic stop.

Judge Taylor was asked during a videotaped question-and-answer session whether it is a clever idea for a person with ASD to carry an ID card. She says that it is but that they should not leave it in the glove compartment or behind the visor, where it can be threatening to a police officer if they see the driver reaching for it. Instead, leave it on the dashboard or somewhere out in the open.

I asked Melissa why she thinks that police officers have been so receptive to her training. She answered,

> More are having experiences with people with ASD. After some sessions we will get emails from some of them asking about people in their jurisdictions. Also, some have family members with ASD. And some have been involved in media situations that have gone bad, so they know they need to learn more about ASD.

I also asked Melissa what she had learned in her previous career as a third-grade teacher that is transferable to her current career working with police, people with ASD, and the criminal justice system. This was her response:

> In the classroom I would turn the lights down, and I learned to be

quiet at times of possible stress. I would speak in short sentences, stay calm, and model the behavior I expected from my students. So I tell police to give people with ASD space, use visuals or things in writing. The three major strategies I recommend, which work effectively with most people but particularly young children or people with ASD, are: (1) time—allow it; (2) space—provide it; and (3) communicate effectively using visuals and written words without reliance on auditory communications.

I suggest that police have sensory bags with items like communication cards, sunglasses to block out light. Some departments are starting to use them.

Melissa also expresses concern that some schools or individual teachers use police as a threat, and this engenders more distrust.

If you have found a particular interest in this chapter, you may want to explore further the work of Judge Taylor; read the books by Nick Dubin, including the one that describes his battle with the legal system; read the chapter of a book coauthored by Melissa and Gary; or read any of the books or articles written by Nick's father, Larry, or the other people quoted in this chapter. All of this and lots more is available via a simple google.

I conclude this chapter with a quote from Vickie Shea:

> Due to cumulative difficulties in understanding what is expected of them or their overstimulation by sensory stimulation in the room, it is rare for a person with ASD to be deliberatively defiant or provocative.

Chapter Fourteen

TEACCH and ABA

You have to put kids in activities they love to do. If they love the little yellow duck, let them color the little yellow duck.

Jennifer Townsend

The two most prominent programs in the field of autism appear to be TEACCH and ABA. Is one better than the other? If one is better, which is it? Is one or the other better depending on the person with autism? This has been one of the more difficult chapters for me to write because of seemingly conflicting opinions I've received from people whom I respect equally.

Clearly there were easy distinctions to be made in the 1980s, when both programs were in their infancy. As the name would imply, the emphasis of applied behavior analysis has traditionally been more behavioral, while TEACCH historically has focused more on seeking to understand what a person with autism is thinking and understanding and using environmental accommodations to build upon the strengths of someone with ASD.

The emphasis of TEACCH is more on individualizing strategies for supporting people with ASD by first seeking to understand what is going on inside their minds. In fact, Eric Schopler's dissertation focused on understanding and supporting the unique learning differences associated with autism, and this focus has remained across the past fifty years of TEACCH. This is often expressed, to again paraphrase Steven Shore, as "to know one person with ASD is to know one person with ASD."

Some of the harshest criticisms of ABA relate to its practices as far back as the 1980s. For instance, Joanne Phillips, Arizona, told me,

> A private school in the area (Deer Valley USD in Arizona) "specialized" in autism, used crude ABA-type practices (forced compliance with negative consequences for undesired behaviors), and treated autism as a mental illness. We brought back our district students who had been placed out of the district into private schools and never should have been because those schools didn't have staff trained in autism.
>
> At Maimonides, as I discovered early in my career, they used a precursor of ABA, and those services were horrible and inhumane. We were told to squirt lemon juice out of water pistols to make students stop screaming, to tie rubber bands around wrists to pull and snap as punishment for not complying, to grasp students' faces to force eye contact, [and] to physically restrain and take down children when they had meltdowns.

Laura Klinger says that both Eric Schopler and Gary Mesibov were strongly against the use of punishment in the treatment of autistic children. They also refrained from using the word "cure" and focused on supporting each person with autism's unique learning differences. As a result of these different philosophical beliefs, TEACCH and ABA were considered to be completely different approaches, with families asked to choose between them when deciding on treatment for their children.

Viviane de Leon says,

> TEACCH and ABA are the most utilized approaches in Brazil, and many children who are autistic are in school, where they receive

clinical treatment. ABA is too reward-based, places too much emphasis on behaviors, and whereas TEACCH seeks to understand why behaviors are what they are, if a child is having a tantrum, ABA would say, "ignore it; don't reward it," while TEACCH would say, "try to understand it from the perspective of the person with ASD." Some evidence supports ABA, but control of behaviors relies too much on compliance.

But are the ABA philosophy and practices the same now as when it was founded in 1968? Barry Prizant has written several books on autism since completing his doctoral work in the mid-seventies at the State University of New York in Buffalo. Barry indicated to me that

> Over the years the approaches of ABA and TEACCH have grown closer, partly because some of the TEACCH innovations such as visual support, schedules, and parents as partners are now accepted as essential, and other programs are even taking credit for what TEACCH originated.
>
> In those early days, the 1970s, there was no such thing as an autistic adult; they were labelled schizophrenics. TEACCH services were there long before others. Today ABA and TEACCH are much more similar, with just slightly different emphases.

However, Svany, in Arizona, takes issue with the notion that ABA and TEACCH are anywhere near similar in their current approaches:

> To say that ABA and TEACCH are growing closer makes no sense to me. The foundation of the approaches are so fundamentally different, especially due to the word "culture," which means autonomy, authenticity, independence, and that is not what ABA stands for; it is about shaping people, keeping them in compliance, and being in control.

Gary was the first person to talk about autism as a culture, which fits very much still today, even more so when so many of our autistic clients are feeling that way and talk about themselves as neurodivergent. Here is how Gary responded each and every time he was asked about ABA versus TEACCH. He would say, "It's very important to understand the depth in TEACCH philosophy, the importance of building relationships and connections with the autistic person and understanding their world. The TEACCH role is to use the interests of people with autism to teach skills but not use them as a reward."

The program of ABA is all built on compliance and control. The comment that TEACCH and ABA approaches are growing closer is so very far from the truth; it is not, in my mind. Gary talked about autism culture and the total acceptance of autistic people. We need to learn about their culture and understand them and not expect them to understand and accept our culture. The TEACCH approach is to listen, support, accept, respect—and never ever any kind of compliance training, which is what ABA is all about.

Kelly Trier also discussed the early days of TEACCH and ABA:

At that time there was a struggle between TEACCH strategies and ABA. The thought was you either used one strategy or the other; you did not use both. The traditional ABA approaches used a discreet trial format, which included lots of drills and practice on skills that were broken down for students. The current thinking is so much more flexible and accepts the use of all strategies that are research based to help students succeed. In this scenario, TEACCH might be said to actually fit into the umbrella of applied behavior analysis.

Jen Townsend has designed a program to draw on the best of ABA and TEACCH. Jen states emphatically,

> One of the strengths of TEACCH is its efforts to avoid prompt dependency. In 2002 my Maryland school district sent me to Chapel Hill for TEACCH training, and my reaction was, "Man, this is like magical training." I could also see value in an applied behavioral analysis approach (ABA) such as discrete trial teaching (DTT), which is an educational strategy based on the principles of applied behavior analysis. However, discrete trial teaching, without consideration [of] the prompt hierarchy and intentionality for transference of skill into naturally occurring routines, can lead to prompt dependency. Discrete trial teaching is good, but prompt dependency is not.
>
> Discrete trial teaching involves breaking skills down into smaller components and teaching those smaller subskills individually. Repeated practice of skills is conducted, and teachers may incorporate prompting procedures, as necessary. Correct responses are followed by reinforcement procedures to facilitate the learning process.
>
> What is a discrete trial? A discrete trial is a single cycle of instruction that may be repeated several times until a skill is mastered. A discrete trial consists of five main parts: (1) an initial instruction (example: "Touch your nose."); (2) a prompt or cue given by the teacher to help the child respond correctly (example: teacher points to child's nose); (3) a response given by the child (example: child touches their nose); (4) an appropriate consequence, such as correct responses receiving a reward designed to motivate the child to respond correctly again in the future (example: "Nice job touching your nose," teacher gives child praise, "good job"); (5) a pause between consecutive trials, waiting one to five seconds

before beginning the next trial (Florida Atlantic University; contact information: website: www.coe.fau.edu/card/).

Because I favored so much of what TEACCH had to offer, I enhanced existing programming to incorporate the TEACCH philosophy with what I felt was good about an ABA approach. Since I felt strongly that prompt dependency was a weakness of an ABA approach and as a result of my experience in Chapel Hill, I focused on "How do you develop a learning program that will encourage people with ASD to function independently?" Gary suggested taking the discrete teaching prompts and putting them into a structured TEACCH approach process. Discrete teaching would tell children when to jump over a puddle, while in a structured work system, I would ask them to tell me what they know about jump.

Once they reach a level of mastering a subskill within learning the skill with prompts, you want to quickly move the child into independence. TEACCH is a master of intrinsic learning. You move children into areas they love to do with encouragement and give them opportunities to be independent. If they love the little yellow duck, let them color the little yellow duck, and then move them into what they need, using their preferences and interests as motivators. Other approaches first want to work their own plans. Gary said, "Put the child first."

The influence Gary had on me was astronomical, and putting the child's interests first was in line with what I believe and just made sense to me.

So what's the answer? Is TEACCH or ABA better for people with autism, or does it depend on the person? Can the two approaches be blended? Has each approach adopted some of the best of the other so that they are much closer philosophically and in practice now than in 1968 and 1972, when ABA and then TEACCH were founded?

Joanne Quinn told me that

Gary didn't try to fit us into a mold. He would say, "You will do with this what is right for you and the community."

Does this mean Gary could support certain ABA practices depending on the circumstances?

My interview with Laura Klinger was one of the last of my many zooms. Laura told me,

The current early intervention programs at TEACCH do combine TEACCH and ABA approaches. More recently ABA has focused on using naturalistic or child-directed approaches in which the therapist follows the child's lead and builds on their interests. Our early intervention program combines the use of discrete trials during therapy from ABA, the use of environmental supports, such as visual supports from TEACCH, and follows the child's interests and strengths, [which] is now advocated by both programs.

Just like TEACCH has incorporated some ABA practices, ABA practitioners have now incorporated some of TEACCH practices. For example, ABA practices now include the use of schedules as pioneered by TEACCH. We'll never use punishment, but most ABA services no longer do. TEACCH still focuses on understanding what the child or adult is trying to communicate and adapting the environment to increase their understanding of the world. As an example, a student may be ripping up papers at his desk; if you look at his environment, you may see that the student only rips when he doesn't know what to do. A more traditional ABA therapist may be focused on the behavior, but really good therapists from both TEACCH and ABA backgrounds don't only look at the behavior; they try to understand the cause. In this case the therapist would try to change the environment to help increase the student's understanding.

The core of TEACCH has always been about looking at the whole child and their specific needs. In the long run, we need to look at the whole child in choosing the best interventions, and that may be ABA and/or TEACCH strategies.

This sounded to me as being consistent with Gary's stated philosophy of tailoring strategies to the specific needs of the individual—and this would allow for the use of strategies from any program.

Laura added,

Traditionally, ABA worked with people one-on-one, while TEACCH focused on changing the environment. But now ABA people talk with teachers about changing the classroom environment, and TEACCH sometimes does one-on-one work. We do whatever it takes to help people with autism understand what's going on around them.

I was starting to get what I thought was the big picture and then it came together completely when Laura said,

I've seen really good and really bad ABA and TEACCH trainers. I've seen an email from a parent who said that her child's teacher never talked because a TEACCH trainer told the teacher, "You shouldn't talk with ASD people." Obviously, this teacher had thought that since people with ASD are generally not auditory learners, it was useless to talk with them at all. This is not at all consistent with TEACCH intervention approaches and was an example of a little bit of information being a dangerous thing.

Laura's observation that there are good and bad trainers helped me understand how the philosophies and practices of the two programs could be somewhat similar in 2022 despite having significantly different philosophies and practices when they were founded. As John Donvan and Caren Zucker point out in their book *In A Different Key*, "Autism was such a rare diagnosis, and so little research had been done on it." Therefore, both programs had little precedent to guide them, and it is logical they could be far apart in their beliefs. As the years went by, each program adapted ideas and approaches from the other. Why wouldn't they since they had the same mission?

So what accounts for the divergence of views between those who believe there are significant differences in the two programs and those who disagree? When Laura commented that there are good and bad people training for both programs around the world, it brought clarity in my mind to the questions relating to the quality of TEACCH and ABA. Whether you believe ABA has adopted some of the best of the TEACCH practices or whether TEACCH uses ABA strategies may depend on the quality of the person implementing the program. In other words, it's possible that the seemingly different assessments of ABA and TEACCH from equally competent people may be due solely to the particular program or practitioner they are witnessing. And no matter how diligent either TEACCH or ABA is in overseeing the people it qualifies to implement its programs, there will be occasions where either program is not being represented at its best. So an opinion of the effectiveness of either program may occasionally be skewed depending on who is representing it.

According to Laura Klinger, the UNC TEACCH autism program addressed the demand for accountability and quality services for individuals with autism spectrum in 2012 when it established a comprehensive certification program to provide educators and clinicians with a professional certification that allows them to document their use of evidence-based practices. This program includes two certification levels, practitioner and advanced consultant.

In any field of expertise, it is logical that widely divergent approaches will come closer together over time. No one has the market on perfection. Good people will always be looking for ways to improve their work, and this is going to include adoption and adaption of their rivals' practices.

My conclusion? It is open to debate as to how similar or different the TEACCH and the ABA approaches are. However, each, as Laura points out, have adopted strategies from the other, so the two approaches are certainly more similar in 2022 than when they were launched about fifty years ago. What is important, to paraphrase what Gary said to Jen Townsend, is to "put the person first."

Chapter Fifteen

Stories Illustrative
of Behaviors

I love the honesty of people with autism; it keeps us
going after a stressful day.

Kelli Bielang

I want to share a misgiving I had telling stories, most of them humorous,
about people with ASD. I needed to understand how you could tell such
stories without mocking them. I knew my brother wouldn't make anyone
the butt of a joke. Yet many of his colleagues had told me that much of his
humor came from injecting stories about people with ASD into his presentations. Also, some of the best stories came from parents of people with
ASD, and surely they wouldn't mock their own children.

As I pondered my concern, two people separately shared thoughts that,
taken together, solved the puzzle for me.

Tomoko compared stories about people with ASD to stories most of us
as parents tell lovingly about our own children, even, at times, our grown
children. The word "lovingly" resonated with me. I immediately thought
of stories my wife Susan and I shared about our children when they were
very young and even now, when they are out of the nest. And I am aware
that as we grow older, our memory lapses and other idiosyncrasies give our

children a repertoire of stories about us. But we tell our recollections lovingly, and we think (hope) their stories about us are told in the same vein.

Catherine Davies completed my education on the subject by pointing out that

> Gary would sometimes share an amusing anecdote of an experience with an individual with autism, never laughing at them but enjoying the situation with them. Whenever Gary told a story about something a person with ASD had said or done, he always explained afterward what we could learn about people with ASD from their behavior that might seem out of the ordinary to us. He would explain that this is a story about social interaction or whatever behavior of an autistic person the story illustrated.
>
> If a student said something funny, Gary would smile to the side with quiet, outgoing appreciation rather than laughing out loud or doing anything that might embarrass the person. He wouldn't reinforce an unusual behavior by laughing at it. In other words, Gary would tell a story, and he would use an unusual behavior that might be funny to many of us as a teachable moment. It's a celebration of the differences in how the individual brain works.

Here are some of the many anecdotes told to me by professionals and parents of children with ASD. The first few illustrate how people with ASD give a literal interpretation to words and phrases that most of us understand are intended figuratively.

From Svany:

> One of my students was attending preparations for his confirmation. The priest says, 'Let's take out the Bible.' The student stands up and starts walking toward the door.

I ask, "Where are you going?"

"He told me to take it out, so I am taking it out," the student replied without the slightest attempt to be funny.

Keith Lovett relates,

Classroom teachers need to realize autistic children will take verbal instructions literally. Gary would tell the story of a teacher who told her students to 'put your hands in,' meaning place your hands in the center of the circle of students. One student got extremely upset thinking he would have to have his arm cut off in order to throw his hands in.

From Cory Shulman:

An ASD person approached me after a presentation and posed a question.

"That's a very good question," I responded. "It will require some time for me to offer an answer. Could we sit on a cup of coffee tomorrow and discuss this?" The young inquirer informed me, in all seriousness, "Don't sit on a cup of coffee. It will be cold, and it will be wet, and it will be very uncomfortable on your backside."

Anne McGuire adds,

If I said, "Oh, that's so sad I was crying my eyes out," a person with ASD might expect to see a pair of eyes falling from my head to the ground. I was once frustrated with myself for forgetting something, and I called myself a 'space cadet.' I was told, "Anne, you are not an astronaut."

Anne also shares this anecdote, as told to her by Gary; it demonstrates the bluntness that can come with a lack of social skills. It is about a young man named Alex (not his real name), who is at least fifty now:

> We often set out snacks for gatherings of our clients but required the students to ask for them before they could have any. It would earn them a snack if they said, 'Cookies, please?' or 'Hand me the bowl' or something similar. Teachers observing in the stands were getting nervous, as the students were unable to get their snacks. Finally Alex, in a burst of frustration, blurted out, "What does a guy have to do to get service around here?"

Jayson Delisle tells of experiences in a car with a client who was typically repetitious:

> Every time I came to a traffic light, the client would say "Jayson, light is red; red means stop. Now it is green; green means go." He didn't mean it as humorous but as a fact that he learned and was told was very important." He also identifies objects and animals and other things along our route: "There's a dog;" "There's another dog"; "There's another dog"; "There's a blue van"; "There's a school bus"; "Look, Jayson, a fire engine"; "Oh look, a Burger King"; "Look, Jayson, see the fountain." We see these same things every day, but he still sees value and meaning in naming them as he sees them. And it is how he socializes with others.

Christina Corsello says,

> Autistic people's honesty can be very funny. They will see us laughing and ask, "What's funny?" So we have to be careful. Gary was good at finding each individual's sense of humor and then adjusting to their style.

Jayson Delisle adds,

> Some people don't like our clients' blunt social style. People some-
> times say autistics don't have a sense of humor. I often say the in-
> dividual is "charming." You have to understand that in many cases,
> they are not trying to be difficult or rude or insensitive, but rather,
> they are just stating the facts as they see them. And when we un-
> derstand their language capacity and communication style, we can
> appreciate the truth in what they say.
>
> But it should not be assumed that if you have autism, you don't
> have a sense humor. Many of my clients do find humor in everyday
> life and derive pleasure from jokes, puns, and absurdist situations.

Keith Lovett relates how

> Gary would take students to football games, and the students
> would often be loud and raucous, flapping their hands, just being
> kids with autism. As the game progressed, most of the fans in the
> crowd were getting progressively more drunk. By the time the game
> was half over, most of the fans were exhibiting the same behavior
> as the students, so Gary's students blended in well with the crowd.

*Keith Lovett and his wife Pam with Gary, 2011 at The University of
Northampton UK during Summer Graduation Ceremonies*

Another TEACCH trainer says,

> One of the clients would go around to delis and grocery stores at the end of each day and would ask, "Will you be throwing away your leftovers?" Each year we had a huge end-of-the-year picnic for TEACCH staff. The day of the picnic, this person collected a macaroni salad, made, of course, with mayonnaise, and put it into the trunk of his car, where it sat (and stewed) until the afternoon, when he put it out with the rest of the food.
>
> Twenty-two of us got food poisoning and were wiped out for the rest of the week. Gary said to the young man, "I think next time you should bring the napkins and paper cups." He wanted to enable the man to make a contribution, since that was what he wanted to do. Gary's comment was an attempt to redirect the autistic person by suggesting a more acceptable way of still following his interest.

Laurie Sperry tells of

> a really big person with ASD who wanted to bring his doll Pebbles (Flintstones) on the bus each day and would march in like a rugby player. We needed to dissuade him from taking his Pebbles on the bus, but Gary often pointed out to us that while redirecting behaviors, we had to honor a person's interests and ideas. He suggested, "What if we set parameters? He can take Pebbles with him when he is out with his mother grocery shopping or when he does certain things, but not on the bus."
>
> "You can't negate the legitimate interests of people with autism," Gary would say.

Cory Shulman tells of Yoni, a little boy in fourth grade, now thirty, whom she describes as bright and intelligent in a regular classroom, maybe the first grade:

He was in a group of eight to work on social skills. At lunch he said, 'I don't want to sit with others at lunch anymore.' It turned out it was the level of noise that bothered him. The other students agreed they wanted him to eat with them, so they suggested he could sit at the teacher's desk, and if it got too loud, he could say 'too loud,' and they would quiet down. Lunches were much quieter after that.

Speaking of Gary's sense of humor, Signe Naftel says,

I picture him knowing that in any conversation, there needs to be some laughter. Working with him was always serious but fun. His humor would relate to what was being discussed, sometimes something humorous our autistic students had said or done.

Lore Gray speaks of a kindergarten or first-grade student who said,

It's so hot in here, my ear wax is melting.

She adds,

How can you not love them?

Lore tells of another young person who said seriously, not intending to be funny,

I'm not racist; I have a black-and-white TV!

Peter Vermeulen tells of a person with ASD who was telling a story and did not like to be interrupted:

When interrupted, he announced, "I don't like to be interrupted." Then he continued telling his story, and Gary interrupted him on purpose. Why?

Gary explained that "Often, people who are with people with ASD are afraid of saying or doing the wrong thing. But when you tease them, you are respecting them and, in effect, saying, "I am me, and I am not going to change because of you."

Here's a story someone told of when Gary was asked for advice by a young man who had a girlfriend but couldn't think of what to do or where to go on a date:

Gary suggested: "Go to the movies; go to a restaurant; go to the beach."
When Gary saw him again, he asked, "How is it going?"
The young man responded, "We broke up."

He had done the three things Gary had told him to do. So he had worked himself through the 'list' Gary had given him, and that was it. This illustrates the need people with ASD have to know when a task is completed or, in this case, when it is not. I'm sure Gary recognized it was his error in not explaining that these three steps did not have to represent the totality of the relationship.

There is one story that offends some people with whom I have shared it. I debated whether to include it but decided that precisely because it can be offensive to some people, it should be shared, because it is an example of how a lack of social awareness can lead to a person with ASD being misunderstood as being rude and insensitive. However, I will add this disclaimer: This story should not be told for any humor one may find in it; it is told as an example of how a person with ASD can unintentionally offend others with an honest comment that someone with social skills might think but would not say out loud.

This was told to me by Susie Schopler, who had heard this from a therapist who was the director of a program in Sweden and was telling about her own personal experience with a client who had autism:

The Swedish therapist was a self-described "elderly and plump woman," and she worked with an especially attractive young assistant. In telling this story, she mentioned that people with ASD often have strength in math and the sciences and think in those terms—and that's what this client was doing:

This autistic student said to me, "I would really love to see you take a bath." I said to the student, "Why would you prefer to see a plump old lady take a bath rather than a beautiful young woman?"

"Because," responded the young student, "I want to see how much water you would displace."

Here are some anecdotes as told by Kelli Bielang from her experiences:

- An elementary student, during recess, which is indoors because it is raining, disappears in the school somewhere. He is caught running around the school. Before his captor can say a word, he asks, "Where was the adult supervision?"

  This demonstrates problems with social cognition and with implicit learning; the student needs to learn to follow the rules.
- During a second-grade math lesson, I asked questions of the young students, and one responded: "Aren't you the teacher? Why are you asking us to do your job?"

  Once again, social cognition and implicit learning.
- A kindergarten student who raised his hand but wasn't one of the first to be called upon shouts out, "Why is she calling on all these other humans?"

  Social cognition.

  I love their honesty. It keeps us going after a stressful day.

How Does One Describe Gary's Sense of Humor?

One of the things that had me stymied was getting a handle on Gary's sense of humor. Almost everyone cited his sense of humor, but few could offer examples. Words like "wry," "dry," and "whimsical" were used, but still no examples. Then I asked Gary to describe his sense of humor, and he said, "spontaneous." And that made sense. Gary's humor was usually situational—a reaction to something someone would say or do. Because of this it was dependent on context, and it wouldn't be funny in a retelling, which is why few can recall examples even as they are saying they enjoyed his sense of humor. In fact, if you tried to retell something Gary said that was humorous at the time, you would probably not get laughs, and you would end up saying, "You had to be there."

Svany described Gary's sense of humor as "sharp and witty."

Cory Shulman says, "Gary has a great sense of humor, much of which [comes] out when he is storytelling."

Here is an example of typical Gary humor: Once in 1975 while Gary was relaxing in a coffee shop following completion of the twenty-six-mile Boston marathon, a fellow runner commented that Bill Rogers had just completed the marathon, setting a record time for an American of 2:09:55. Acting unimpressed, Gary commented, "So Rogers was only out there a little more than two hours. I ran for almost five hours. I'd like to see him match that."

Lee Marcus observes, "

Gary's humor was never nasty or critical but often silly. If he was with people not aligned with his principles or the principles of TEACCH, he could articulate in ways that showed no rancor.

Laurie Sperry offers another example of Gary's humor:

We were in NYC doing a training, and we happened to be in the same hotel where they were filming a toddler beauty pageant. A number of fussy toddlers in full makeup, hair sprayed into helmets, and wearing uncomfortable outfits got onto the elevator with us. When they got off the elevator, Gary said, "We should hand out our cards the next time because they'll all need therapy at some point."

Cory Shulman says,

> An amazing characteristic of Gary's humor, which I would charac-
> terize as "dry," so you don't sit there and laugh out loud, is that it is
> part of his personality. He occasionally told a few jokes. More likely
> he would tell a few stories that would make us laugh. His attitude
> was you need to smile to enjoy life.
>
> Someone in an audience once said of a comment by a person
> with autism, "Oh, that was so rude."
>
> Gary responded, "Rude? Let me tell you a story about manners.
> One client always would ask women how much they weighed. The
> client and I went to the dictionary and looked up the definition
> of manners. The client then said, 'I don't like manners; it's lying.'"
>
> Gary said to the audience, "You know what? He was right."
> That was not the response we expected. Gary used stories to teach
> strategies.

Susanne Hvidtfeldt and Regnar Hintze Thisted described Gary's sense of
humor:

> You have to know him a little. It's difficult to find the right words
> to describe his sense of humor. It seems to come through in the
> situation. Something happens, and Gary has a comment which
> makes you smile or laugh and makes you feel good inside.

Speaking of Gary's sensitivity to people from different cultures, Steve
Kroupa said,

> Gary had a good sense of humor. During his lectures he would
> make us laugh. English doesn't always translate easily into Japanese,
> and some speakers from other countries would make an attempt
> at humor, and no one would laugh. Gary seemed to be able to

inject humor into his stories that Japanese people would understand. Probably this was partly due to Gary being careful about the translators he would select, and he would use the same ones each time once he got to know them.

Gary told me that

a translator, not for him, once said that jokes don't translate well in some languages. In his native language, this translator told the audience, "The person speaking is telling a joke, so when I am finished talking and pretending to translate, please laugh."

Laurie Sperry added,

We would go to camp for a weekend each year with the adult autism group, and even though he was this world-famous man, Gary would go to camp with us. He would play the silly games right alongside everyone else. On the last day of camp, he would sit around with everyone and sing, "leavin' on a jet plane/don't know when I'll be back again.

Keith Lovett describes Gary's humor as "dry" humor;

Gary understood English humor, which many Americans don't. Many Americans take things literally, and a lot of English humor is based on double entendre. Gary obviously knew how to get an audience laughing because he knew his lectures had to be spiced up to keep people interested—he did this with humor, videos, and PowerPoint.

Lee Marcus:

Gary has a whimsical sense of humor, and it would surface in the context of what we were doing; he would say something that was not what you would expect. He would be funny in social situations with clients, and he would match the level of his humor to the cognitive level to the people he was with in any group, sultans or others.

Peter Vermeulen recalls Gary's sense of humor as British: "kind, wry, not banana or slapstick, more refined."

Anne McGuire says,

> Gary had a very dry sense of humor that reflected his intellect. He was a gifted speaker. He told stories about people with autism but never made fun of them.

Susan Moreno met Gary in Georgia:

> I was asked to speak, and there were lots of important people there to also speak. We were in a church, and my whole family is small; I wouldn't have been able to see over the podium. Normally I would walk to the side of the podium with the microphone; however, they were taping the presentations, and the one stationary camera was focused on the podium. Someone found a box for me to stand on. I forgot I was on the podium, and at the end of my presentation, I stepped on air and fell unceremoniously to the ground. I was sore from the experience, but nothing was broken. The next day I laughed at how stupid I felt I had been. Gary was there for my presentation, but we still hadn't met.
>
> We finally got together at a conference in Eugene, Oregon. Gary approached me after my presentation and offered a humorous comment about my experience on the podium. Sometime after I had returned home, I was called to the phone and told it was

Gary Mesibov. I thought it was a friend playing a joke, because we often did play jokes on each other. I picked up the phone and said, "Hi, Gary, sweetie, baby."

He said, "We want you to come to North Carolina and present." And he said that after I had been to North Carolina, he would want me to write a chapter for a book. And I kept responding to him with "OK, deary," and "Yes, I hear you, sweetie."

Then he said, "And when you come down here, we don't want you to fall off the podium." Since I hadn't told anyone else about that, I realized it was actually Gary.

I went to Chapel Hill and learned that usually at these conferences, only three people spoke, and they all had their doctorates. Then I overheard Eric asking Gary why he had invited someone who was not a doctor, so I really felt I didn't belong, and I spoke to Gary. He told me that Eric could occasionally be a little bit of a stuffed shirt, but that after he heard me speak, he was sure Eric would appreciate what I had to offer.

In order to relax me, Gary added, "We fixed it so you can't fall off the podium." Afterward, to his credit, Eric did come up to me, told me he appreciated what I had to offer, and said sincerely that he was looking forward to reading my chapter. Gary, as had Eric before him, recognized that parents had an expertise with autism that others did not have, even if Gary took it to another level of having them present on panels with professionals in the field. Also, it should be remembered that while Eric might have initially resisted having someone without a doctorate be a presenter, it was he who first wrote about the need to treat parents as partners with the medical people.

Dr. Lorna Wing was in her seventies when she spoke at this conference. She tripped coming off the podium, and the audience gasped, except for Gary and me; we exchanged smiles. I didn't want her to think we were being insensitive, so I approached her, and she turned her back to me with her hand to her chin, reflecting the stereotypical British coolness as I spoke. I explained how I had tripped coming off the podium in Oregon, and that it was because of this [that] Gary and I had exchanged smiles, not because we were laughing at her for falling.

Slowly she turned around to face me and then broke into hysterical laughter. "That's the funniest thing I ever heard," she said.

Catherine Davies says,

In my experience, Gary tended to have a more reserved sense of humor. He would sometimes share an amusing anecdote of an experience with an individual with autism, never laughing at them but enjoying the situation with them. He would also utilize these examples to illustrate the culture of autism to attendees during trainings, making it a teachable moment. I think many of us that work in this field share these stories because we enjoy experiencing the different ways that individuals with autism think (by which I mean, different from our own thinking).

So now I have enough to describe Gary's sense of humor: spontaneous/situational, woven into his storytelling, sometimes silly, and often self-deprecating. The last word goes to Gary's daughter-in-law, Sally, who characterizes his sense of humor as "corny jokes. I used to roll my eyes skyward, but now I think they're funny."

Chapter Sixteen

Eric Schopler and Gary Mesibov: Unassuming Experts

Gary and Eric are the history of TEACCH.

Lore Gray

Part One: Eric Schopler

Eric Schopler

Haven't you known people who can be somewhat withdrawn in most situations but behave like the king or queen in their castle when you are with them in their own home? Eric's home, figuratively, was anything connected to his work on autism as well as his actual home when he was with his family. This is how I reconcile two observations from his first wife, Betsy (1953–1970). On the one hand, Betsy told me that Eric was somewhat insecure owing to his childhood experiences in Nazi Germany and the need for his family to flee to America when he was eleven years old. However, I asked Betsy if he would be stressed during the times such as 1969, when the money was about to run out, and he had no guaranteed funding to continue his work. "Not at all," she said. "He knew what he was doing was right and that it would be recognized."

Eric was quite secure with his work and in his family environment. I believe that work and his home environment were the equivalent of "home" to him in the sense that when he was involved in his work with autism, or he was with his family, he was playing on his home field. His three children all speak of Eric as a devoted father who always put them first.

I asked Gary why he and Eric had been so successful as collaborators. I was more interested in how their personalities meshed, since it was apparent they had shared values and interpreted autism research similarly. They both set precedents for treating parents as partners, not as clients of the professionals. "You'll never find a parent sitting in the waiting room while her child is being examined," Laura Klinger told me.

Eric and Gary both fought internal university battles to protect the independence of their program and to maintain its priority providing support to families of people with autism. Eric won the important battles; Gary did, too, including his most important one in 2009, the year he retired as Director of TEACCH to be succeeded by Laura Klinger a year later.

According to Tom Schopler, he and Gary made certain that the TEACCH program would retain its ability to function independently within the university system, despite attempts to place TEACCH under the supervision of a department Gary feared would change the nature of the program. Also, it was about a year later when, according to Tom, the university chancellor ordered that $60,000 be restored to the TEACCH budget from another department when an audit Tom had encouraged the Chancellor to seek revealed that this amount was part of an endowment that was earmarked exclusively for the TEACCH program.

Each of these pioneers, Eric and Gary, inspired trust and confidence from people with ASD and their parents. In Japan and many other countries, each is considered a hero in the field of autism comparable to the degree that the Beatles are heroes in the field of entertainment.

Eric, as described by his son Tom, was more of a visionary who left the details to others. Gary was also a visionary but perhaps better with the details. Both knew how to get done what they wanted done.

Gary recently explained to me why he felt they worked so well together:

> Eric could be a little brisk or abrupt. He didn't intentionally intimidate people, but TEACCH staff members were sometimes intimidated by his reputation and his manner. My interpersonal skills might have been a bit better. Although I hasten to add that Eric could charm people when he wanted to, and people with ASD, as well as their family members, never felt intimidated by him.

There was certainly nothing intimidating about the way Eric dressed or carried himself. One coworker said he would come into the office having just come from working in the field at his farm, and sometimes the bottoms of his shoes would provide evidence of where he had been. Another person said, with a friendly smile, that Eric could at times fit the stereotype of the absent-minded professor, forgetting his passport, or not having every button and zipper where it should be while he was presenting.

Andy Short tells of Gary coming to the program with a special focus on adults and adolescents:

He was applying the same principles as Eric and the TEACCH program; however, TEACCH had not yet focused as much on adolescents, so Gary added a new dimension. Eric's focus was autism itself and the causes and treatments, whereas Gary came to Chapel Hill with little exposure to autism but a great deal of understanding of adolescent psychology."

Eric's children portray him as a wonderful father. His older son Bobby told me,

He was a father who never let his work get in the way of responding affirmatively if we suggested we go fishing or the like. When he was home, he always had dad time to play a game of cards or help us with whatever we were doing. Family was so important to him, and it always took precedence. "Hey, Dad, do you want to go fishing?" we might ask while he was racing to complete a paper by a deadline.

Tom said,

If you were pushing our dad, he would push back. But he'd always listen. He could get mad. We suppose he could be intimidating, but not to us and not intentionally to anyone else. People were always welcome in our home. At home or at work, he always dressed in corduroys or jeans. He was not one to care too much for physical appearance.

Tom recalls that what made their father's work unique was that

He created a generalist model; in the past there was little coordination among specialists, and there were specialists for all different aspects of illness, disease, et cetera. There were psychologists, speech therapists, occupational therapists. Eric created a team of generalists who worked together and among them covered the areas of different specialists.

Dad's interviews for new hires always included parent interviews of the potential employees. Also, our father got many people out of institutions and into homes.

As children our dad would ask us to participate in tests and then give us M&M's as a reward for participating. For instance, he might ask us to reach into a bag and feel an object and describe what it is.

Bobby added,

I didn't realize how great my father was and how much of an impact he had around the world until I was in my twenties, because when he was home, he was home.

Tom and I went to Schmallenberg, Germany, for the opening of a group home to be named *The Eric Schopler House,* named in his honor by the Organization of Social Work Saint George. He was getting all these awards posthumously.

Tom added that

My first wife, Janet Martin, a therapist who continues to travel the world as a TEACCH trainer, had made it clear to me what a big deal my dad was. After his death it became clear to us as Bobby went to New Orleans and I went to Norway to accept awards in his honor. He was receiving awards and commendations from all over the world. The award in Norway was a lifetime achievement award from the International Society of Autism.

In Norway after I spoke, people were coming up to me and saying, "You don't know the impact your father had on my life."

Originally my stepmother was going to represent him in Norway—
this was shortly after he had died—and she asked me to go with
her. However, she died before the trip, so I went. It was a humbling
experience because of the parents who came up to me after my
speech.

Dr. Sasaki in Japan tried to get him nominated for a Nobel
Prize for his work on autism; the Japanese felt so strongly about
his work there. I feel a great sense of pride in his accomplishments.
Essentially he revolutionized the whole approach to autism. He
was good at letting people use their strengths.

David Lashley was one of Dad's original successes. At age six
he was nonverbal and not potty trained. Within six years he was
playing Oliver in *Oliver Twist*.

Viviane de Leon reports that

Eric and Gary were both very close to their clients. Neither imposes
any distance with us or the families. They were very respectful of
everyone, and they used a lot of examples of people with ASD to
help others understand who they were and how to improve their
quality of life. And they taught us to respect people with ASD, and
they taught us to work with families of people with ASD.

Steve Kroupa says,

One of the highest compliments ever paid to Gary was from Eric
Schopler at Eric's retirement party, attended by more than three
hundred people. I'm not exactly sure of the number, but there are
videos of the event, and Alice Wertheimer helped to organize it.
Eric said, "Hiring Gary to be the next TEACCH director is the
best decision I have ever made."

Eric works with a child

Part Two: Gary Mesibov

Gary was experiencing early stage Alzheimer's when I first interviewed him for this book, but he had clear recollections of some events in the past, and this is some of what he told me:

> Eric Schopler was already a legend in the field of autism when I came to UNC in 1973. He had carved out a niche for himself supervising child psychology but working mostly, himself, with children. My focus on adolescents and my degrees in child psychology made for a powerful partnership with Eric, [with] each of our strengths complimenting the other's less familiar backgrounds. Eric's strength was psychology and autism in general.
>
> Some have credited me with being strong on interpersonal relations, saying that I had inherited certain traits from my mother. I always described my mother to others as one who could go into the

bathroom in a public place and come out able to tell you the life history of anyone she met in there.

I guess I had a little of Mom in me: polite, easygoing, and stuff like that. I could get along with people that others could not. Eric, on the other hand, was very smart and abrupt. Eric brought his reputation and knowledge to our work; he enjoyed being the ornery, tough-guy type. When I began working with him, he appeared to me, young as I was, to be nearing the end of an illustrious career. I probably thought he was in his seventies, when in reality, he hadn't reached age fifty.

A lot of people were scared of Eric. My strength was I wasn't afraid of him. He couldn't work with me-too people. I recognized his talent and skill. He liked working with me because he knew I wasn't afraid of him. He had grant funds, so he created his own island, not as a department head obligated to those above him in the hierarchy.

As a graduate student, initially I did most of his leg work. He paid for me. In the second year, I said, "I'd like to continue this work." He said he'd be glad to continue my funding. Eventually the UNC department picked me up (1977), possibly through an autism grant.

Gary spent his first year of college at Rutgers University in New Jersey. He probably chose Rutgers because Fred, a very close cousin, had gone to Rutgers on a basketball scholarship, and also, it was about a three-hour drive from our home, which was a good distance—not too close, not too far.

Gary told me why he decided to transfer to Stanford after his freshman year:

When I applied to college, I wasn't sure of what I wanted to do and probably didn't give enough thought to it. On a visit home from Rutgers, I was at a party with some of my high school friends, and it was like listening to a repeat of the same old stories and the same old jokes, except we were older now. Nothing seemed to have changed from high school; so I said to myself, "I need to grow up."

Before starting his junior year at Stanford, Gary applied to be the roommate of a polio victim who was mostly paralyzed, and according to Gary,

> The only thing he could do was hold a pen in his right hand and move it around. He had to be in the natural sciences so he could push his answers to test questions. He received a lot of support from his accomplished family. I think his mother was the first woman to graduate from Duke Law School.
>
> I had to be his personal nurse, dress him, feed him, and do all the things necessary under the circumstances. The position came with a stipend, and I applied for the role for two reasons: (1) I wanted to see if I was skilled and had the disposition to work with someone with a handicap, and (2) I felt guilty about having our parents pay the expensive tuition at Stanford, and I wanted to offset their cost to some degree.

Here are two fun facts: Gary spoke with a measure of pride about his participation in the early 1950s trial program to assess the Salk polio vaccine. He later learned he was given the actual vaccine, not the placebo. Then in 1964 Gary sold hot dogs at the World's Fair in New York.

Following three years and a bachelor's degree in child psychiatry from Stanford, he and Laurie married in August 1967, after which Gary received a master's degree from the University of Michigan. Then they spent three years in Guam, where Gary and Laurie both taught. They initially signed up for two years and then extended a year because they were enjoying the experience so much; they loved the people in Guam.

I recall that part of their motivation in going to Guam was the exemption from being drafted that was provided because of a shortage of teachers there. Gary doesn't recall that, although he says that might have been part of the reason. It is vivid in my mind because our grandmother, who rarely ventured out of her home in West Hempstead and equally as rarely paid attention to the news, listened constantly to the radio at that time to see if the war had ended and the risk of Gary being drafted had lessened.

Here's a timeline of Gary's career:

1963 Graduated West Hempstead High School (Long Island, NY)
1967 Graduated Stanford University
1968 Master's degree University of Michigan
1968–1971 Guam, teaching
1971–1972 Doctorate at Brandeis University
1973–1977 Postdoctoral work at UNC supervised by Eric Schopler and funded by grants
1977–1993 Assistant Director of TEACCH
1977–2012 Professor at UNC
1993–2009 Director of TEACCH
2012–2018 Independent consultant until a serious problem walking (and traveling) caused full retirement

If I were asked to name people who might give sincere testimony about what a wonderful person I am, I'd be pleased if I could think of ten; it might have been twelve when our parents were alive. Well, I can now count eighty-three people who have personally given such testimony to me about Gary, and they have backed up their affection and admiration for him with a myriad of examples. Many have then followed up our conversation with emails adding information they thought of after we had ended our Zoom.

In each of these eighty-three conversations, one of my many questions was, "How would you describe Gary?" I gave no other prompts. Repeatedly, the words used to describe Gary were "kind," "generous," "patient," "respectful," and "articulate."

Mary Beth Van Bourgondien says,

> Gary was my supervisor, and I worked closely with him. He placed a lot of trust in people he worked with. He hired competent people and recognized their strengths and encouraged them. He has trained many of us across the world, such that his contributions continue to spread and touch the lives of many.

Kathy Hearsey adds,

> Gary was a no-frills person, very practical and pragmatic, who was vested in supporting individuals with ASD and their families. As a leader in the field of autism, he helped to build a workforce that valued the culture of autism and implemented visual strategies and supports to help individuals with autism develop independence, competence, and confidence. He recognized that it would take a village, and he helped to build that village by developing professional training programs, presenting at conferences around the world, and mentoring undergraduate and graduate students who went on to build successful careers in the field of autism.
>
> Gary encouraged each of us to pursue our passion and valued the programs and intervention strategies that were developed from these pursuits. He was an amazing mentor who provided me and my colleagues with opportunities to grow professionally as clinicians and trainers. He provided meaningful and constructive feedback with a kind and positive focus. He didn't simply tell you what you could do to improve; he helped you to identify

areas of personal growth, and provided guidance throughout the process, often sharing his own experiences to make a personal connection.

Cathy Lord thinks back to 1976:

> I was an intern in the DDC (Development Disorder Center) program at UNC. Gary was my supervisor. He was wonderful. Gary did assessments, which is what DDC did, but he focused on follow-up. He was good at seeing what [was] going on and how to help. He was also good at finding something positive in people. He could not only say it, but he was good at getting you to show your strengths.
>
> Gary was consistently kind and creative. He was good at thinking out of the box in terms of how we [could] help this family. If this kid [was] coming home from school and fighting with their parent until dinnertime, what [could] we do to help this child get a social network and keep busy until dinnertime?
>
> Gary was unique—so perceptive at getting to the core of an issue. He wanted to know, "What is the core issue here?" He wanted to mitigate the conflicts (he called them "minor issues") that naturally occurred between parents of autistic children and their children without rewarding the children for obnoxious behavior. For example, "How do we help parents understand this from the child's perspective?"

Kara Hume says,

> Roger Cox and I traveled to many countries to do training, and we visited sites usually where Gary had been, and I could see the results. Gary had a worldwide impact, which one can see just from the number of countries he visited. In Israel his books were translated for cultural adaptation purposes into Hebrew, where reading is right to left.
>
> Gary is like a celebrity all over the world. I know that whenever

he went to Japan, people wanted their photo with him. When I went in his stead in 2020, everyone was asking about him. Gary had international reach in terms of the number of people around the world he mentored.

Gary often showed us how people with ASD think, but he would tell us how we could do something about it. He would ask how we could be more responsive to their needs, how we could make adjustments to accommodate them. I benefited from relationships he passed along to his successor, Laura Klinger, and then she passed along to me. A lot of that was his generosity. A lot was his willingness to share. He wanted what needed to be done to be done whether he was involved or not.

He was incredibly generous personally and intellectually. He made everyone feel valued and important. He was always interested in our work. I feel like Gary was TEACCH.

Viviane de Leon says,

Gary, especially, was very close to the parents. There was a very human side to him; he would share dinnertime with the parents. Gary also was very worried about adolescents and adults when they got older and what kinds of support we could offer them."

Heather Delisle adds,

It's amazing how many lives my husband, Jayson, has touched over his twenty-eight years with this program. I met Gary in 1997 at a sleepaway retreat for forty to sixty clients at Camp Royall in Pittsboro, North Carolina. I knew Gary was a big man in autism, the captain steering the ship. He was important but was unassuming and very easy to talk with.

Everyone was expecting Gary would be coming this day, and

they were excited. I was sitting by a pond, on the grass, and Gary came over and sat next to me, and introduced himself. He was so understanding, kind, and unassuming, but he wasn't intimidating.

Joanie Berry, Gary's secretary for fifteen years, says,

Gary had such an upbeat personality with everyone, even people he barely knew. As stressed as he must have been at times, I don't recall any time he didn't come into the office with a smile and warm greeting and a "How'd you like that game last night?" I never met anyone so kind and considerate.

Catherine Davies says,

Gary clearly cared a lot about individuals with autism, their families, and the people attending the training. Those trainings were very intense, and the pace could be stressful. Gary would always be a calming presence supporting us in our work, even if we were overwrought. He would also make time to interact with the students with autism and ensure that they had a good experience during the training.

Christina Corsello says,

Gary was one of my interviewers when I initially applied for the internship in 1993. When I started my internship, he supervised my adult cases. When I arrived for the initial interview as an intern applicant, as I approached his office I thought to myself, "Oh my, he's written all these books and articles, and he is director of this program." I was immediately struck by his humility and unassuming personality. I knocked on his office door, and he opened it and immediately made me feel comfortable. He gave me a warm greeting and was so kind and gracious. He treated me as a friend, and we had a discussion, not a formal meeting.

He didn't use his desk as a shield and a reminder that we were at different levels positionally. He wore tennis shoes with his dress slacks. Gary is someone that I have great admiration for and who has influenced me greatly, both personally and professionally.

Gary was an incredible mentor. He made you think about things in a different way and with soft-spoken questions and counsel. I told him of one student who would go into town and loved to collect papers of any kind. He would go to Kinko's and Staples and places that would have papers to discard, and he would collect them. I asked Gary, "How do I create alternative strategies to transition this student to more appropriate behaviors?"

Gary didn't suggest that I not try to transition this student away from collecting papers, but he simply informed me that "others have tried strategies to change this student's behaviors with paper but without any luck." He made it clear that it was OK with him if I tried, but he also wanted me to know that the community and individual with autism also need to be considered. He had a very practical approach. When I said, "He can't just take papers," he said, "Well, the truth is that it seems he can."

The idea of respecting a person's interests and strengths and not always just trying to change behaviors was something that Gary always focused on, and the field is just starting to shift to this way of thinking. Gary can take something complex, and he could see both sides and take a balanced approach.

Gary taught me to identify strengths and weaknesses and to think about my strengths as I presented. He said to me, "You are an excellent presenter. You are so good at articulating your thoughts, and you process information quickly." He also told me that I can be impatient sometimes, as I expect others to also process quickly and articulate their ideas. He shared that this was something to pay attention to, and I have ever since. His observation was astute, and he conveyed it in a supportive manner that I could hear and learn from.

He had a way of offering feedback that made you feel good while still receiving his message.

Anne Haeussler calls Gary

very kind, very unassuming, approachable, and competent. Over the years I always felt he is such an important person, but he always stayed in touch and wrote kind notes and never made me feel uncomfortable. TEACCH and Gary have always been so much more about respect than anything else; he has respect for clients, colleagues, and everyone.

Gary always saw the potential in people. He was always willing to see the perspective of other people. Where others might propose something that was inconsistent with TEACCH principles, Gary would say, "Well, maybe there are some people who would benefit from this." I learned never to dismiss a contrary opinion entirely.

Outside the program people placed the highest value on the materials. Gary taught us that the TEACCH program philosophy has to do with how we think and how we treat and value people and respect differences.

Mike Chapman tells of a woman with autism who had an amazing relationship with Gary:

She would believe anything he told her. If I told her something, she would run to Gary and ask him the same question, and when he gave her the same answer, she would thank him as if I hadn't said it. When Gary spoke, they listened. He was able to develop an unbelievable trust with his clients. Where they might not respond to our prodding to do something, all he had to do was say, "Why don't you try this?"

Cory Shulman also speaks of Gary's respect, saying,

Gary has respect for everyone; he is committed to making sure the world is the best it can be and in making it even better. He sees everyone for what they are and focuses on their strengths, not their deficits. If someone had 60 percent bad behaviors and 40 percent good behaviors, he would focus on the 40 percent good behaviors."

David Preece concurs, saying,

Many professionals like to come in like a firefighter and spray the water and then leave without caring what caused the fire. But you can't put out the fire and never know what caused it. Instead you have to be a detective and find the cause in order to determine the solution. Gary never exhibited any defensiveness. He might say, "OK, that's what I didn't expect to happen, but let's figure out why." He was very interested in the well-being of people, but more so, how to help people get the most out of life.

Brigitte Nelles told me,

Gary was the most inspiring person I met relating to autism. What always impressed me about Gary was how open-minded he was to the differences among people with autism. His curiosity to discover more and more about their thinking and their logic has always been an incitement to go further and to question our social rules. Learning the differences among people with autism was an adventure and fun; it was a challenge.

Tom Galperin recalls Gary as being

> always kind and approachable. No ego there whatsoever. We had all these visitors from around the world who thought he was the greatest, someone they idolized; he was so revered. But to me he continued to just be Gary. He always wore his tennis shoes to work. The tennis-shoe thing always cracked me up; here was this super revered guy who just casually wore tennis shoes to work. To this day I have always worn running shoes to work; I was always a causal dresser, and Gary sort of gave me a model that being casual with dress was OK. I'm not sure I've ever told anyone that before.
>
> Whenever I went to him with a request, he never said no. If he was having trouble with my request, he might say "Let me think about it." But he'd always get back to me, and if he couldn't be comfortable approving my request completely, he would always find parts that he could approve. He never said, "That's not going to happen." Even though he was Gary, informal and approachable, he still scared the hell out of me. He was this giant in the field of autism and so widely respected and revered. Even though he did everything possible to make me feel comfortable, I was still scared when we would meet.

Melissa Sreckovic, who only met Gary a few years ago as an intern at TEACCH, says that

> The best advice I ever received in academia was from Gary. When I was seven months pregnant with my son Luka, I was applying for jobs. I got a job interview at Michigan State University. I was excited and nervous. I went to Gary's office, and I said, "Gary, they are never going to hire me if they know I am pregnant" (and trust me, there was no hiding that I was pregnant!). He said, "Melissa, if

they don't want to hire you because you are pregnant, do you really want to work there?"

From that moment forward, I had a different mindset when applying for jobs. On my first on-campus interview, I talked about my son to several people. I wanted to make sure that I found a job where I could put my family first, and Gary's advice gave me the courage to do that. I landed a job at a university that is family friendly.

Gary was an excellent mentor. He taught me so much about autism and the criminal justice system, and my experiences working with him and learning from him really shaped my career. I will be forever grateful that he supported me as a graduate student and mentored me during the early years of my career.

Laura Klinger recalls her first contact with Gary between 1987 and 1990:

I was struggling with what to do with this case. Someone suggested, "talk with Gary." "Right," I said. "Will the director of TEACCH even talk with me?" Gary sent me a ton of resources within twenty-four hours of my calling him. He would even exchange emails with graduate students he didn't know."

Svany says,

I love the way Gary talks about enthusiasm as opposed to obsessive- compulsive behavior. If you say something negative, like "obsessive-compulsive behavior," Gary will say, "You mean enthusiasm." I truly value my friendship with Gary. He was always so generous and always willing to help. Over the years I would call him many times for advice regarding difficult situations. He was great about writing back with questions; he would respond to a question with a question and make me think it through again. It always worked."

Jen Townsend agrees:

> I never felt Gary was talking over or at you. He was talking with you.

Alice Wertheimer says,

> Gary hired me to answer the phones because he wanted a parent to be the first person parents of children with ASD spoke with to set their minds at ease. Also, I spoke several languages and had traveled abroad considerably. He saw something in me that he believed would be great for his program. It was his strength to put people in positions where they could be successful and that would be great for the program.

Kaia Mates recalls a January 1989 trip to Japan:

> Our team included Kathy Hearsey, who was six months pregnant; I had a three-month-old daughter, and we brought along a sitter for her, and Eric, in his last few years as director, was with us.
>
> We brought training to Japan; Gary made sure we were well taken care of. He would invite us by saying, "You want to come along to take our training model to Japan?"
>
> I went with Gary in the 1990s to Karachi, Pakistan, when they were bombing hotels, Kuwait when people were grateful to the United States but were still checking for bombs under cars, and to Northern Ireland when things were scary. Gary told us we would be safe. He trusted the people who invited and made arrangements for us. These were people who begged him to come.
>
> In Pakistan I had bodyguards on both sides of me, and we were not allowed out of our hotel. We also traveled to Singapore and

Taiwan. Gary would tell me the risk wasn't that bad. But I'd look at the State Department website, where they would warn against travel to some of these places. Gary was very protective of us. He would walk me to my room at the hotel and did what he could to be sure we were always safe. We were in a working partnership, even though he was the boss.

Gary particularly couldn't resist parents who would beg him for advice and training. If there were parents desperate for services in the United States or overseas, Gary would bring them to the Chapel Hill Center. Also, as he traveled the world, if someone said, "I have a child and need diagnostic services," we would bring in those people to Chapel Hill; in fact, Gary would bring in people from around the world to build funding for the program, if they had enough money to travel to America.

Gary gave me my hands-on experiences in training teachers, parents, and staff so when I lectured, I had something real to talk about. He had access to postdoctoral students, interns, et cetera that he could utilize to form a team for the diagnostic work. This helped him bring in dollars for TEACCH. Whenever there was a team for any of our work, Gary was always part of that team. Kathy and I were loyal and close to Gary. We were his go-to people, along with a few others.

In my estimation Gary was at the top of the autism pile. I personally think his greatest contribution was developing a training program that trained people all over the world to understand what autism (ASD) is and what are useful strategies that can be used in homes by parents and in educational settings to enhance and improve lives of folks with ASD.

Susan Moreno observed that

Gary always handled everything with common sense, kindness, and a focus on why we were here for whatever was our task. By 1989 he already had connections at colleges to support high-performing people on the spectrum. Two ways to describe him: compassionate and one of the finest gentlemen I have ever known.

Signe Naftel credits Gary with

being the person who very much shaped who I am professionally. He supervised my dissertation weekly and provided countless opportunities for his university students, and he wrote outstanding letters of recommendations, some of which gained me admittance into programs. He was known all over the world in terms of autism. He was so relatable, easy to talk with, very approachable, very friendly.

Cathy Pratt says,

In all my interactions with Gary, I found him to be a kind and humble man. He clearly valued the people he served and put their interest first. Gary's impact can be felt across the world. His life-changing work has changed so many lives, including mine. Gary really cares about individuals with autism, people he trains, and their families. He was always calm and measured. There is a lot of stress dealing with people and issues of autism, but you could trust Gary to keep his head when others were too stressed out. I've even known professionals elsewhere to lose their cool and yell at us if they didn't like our questions.

Gary's kindness and generosity really came through at times we'd be training, and during a break, I would likely see him in a corner communicating with a person with autism instead of collaborating with leaders as you might expect.

David Preece adds,

> Gary was very interested in the well-being of people, but more so
> how to help people get the most out of life. He was interested in
> how animals help people learn. Around 2010 he spoke to me about
> a service dog idea, but I never really knew that much about it other
> than he'd put plans together to work with some folks back in North
> Carolina regarding the use of service animals in service to people
> with autism and their well-being."

Joanne Quinn says,

> Gary was such an integral part of my son's life and mine for many
> years.

Lore Gray calls Gary

> a mensch, intelligent, and he has a gift for giving. He has humane
> treatment for and towards everyone, not just individuals with au-
> tism. He is not at all self-impressed, and he is generous. Gary and
> Eric are the history of TEACCH. He was a very sweet part of my
> life. And this is why I'm sure 95 percent of the people he met loved
> him. So many other professionals talk in high-tech language. Gary
> speaks so clearly, everyone can understand him. He puts the re-
> search into doable strategies.

Marie Howley claims,

> Gary was extremely popular with families. Many would say he was
> the first one they'd spoken with about their child's situation that
> they could really understand. He had humility and empathy.

Marie Howley with her twin children, age 3, in 1999

Barry M. Prizant says,

> Gary truly was one of the voices of integrity and dedication in a field that has always been so divisive and inflammatory. In fact, over the years, myself and my colleagues have spoken many times at the TEACCH conferences, and we have contributed at least two or three chapters to the Schopler and Mesibov book series.

Andy Short adds,

> Another thing that always impressed me was how he spoke to an audience in a nice, relaxed, soft-spoken, unpretentious way, as if he were talking with each person to an audience of one. I would occasionally cover for Gary when he was travelling, and that gave me a sense of how loyal and devoted his clients were to him and him to them. If I gave them advice, they would ask, "Is this what Gary would say?"

Linda Watson, a former TEACCH research associate, relates that,

I had completed six years working on my doctoral thesis at Boston University in 1979 when TEACCH received a grant to work on communications and social skills. Paula Minion was at BU and connected me with Eric Schopler, and the result was that I moved to Chapel Hill to work on the grant.

We had a request from Northside Residence School in Georgia for a consultation focused on students with language problems. Gary handed this off to me. I had never been a consultant before. I went and spoke with parents, staff members, administrators, and others connected with the school.

When I returned to UNC, I met with Gary, and I said to him that it was apparent to me that every group had its own agenda, and I wanted advice on how to proceed. Gary asked, "Who's paying you?"

"The parent association," I replied. "Then that's your agenda," he told me. When he said it, it seemed so obvious, but I hadn't thought of it.

Family always came first with Gary. Occasionally some people might even have been a little annoyed because Gary would cancel a meeting in order to be in Charlotte with Brian when Brian was working there as an attorney.

Vickie Shea says,

I recall one time—it must have been 1975 because Laurie was in the hospital having Todd, so Brian would have been four years old. Gary and I took Brian to McDonald's for food for all of us and discussion time for Gary and me. We were done eating, and Gary and I wanted to continue our discussion, so Gary peeled a small part of the wrapper off a straw and handed it to Brian. "Brian, could you do me a favor, please, and take this to the garbage can at the other end of this room?" When Brian returned, having fulfilled his chore, Gary had another piece of the wrapper ready for Brian to take to the garbage. It was a game that Brian enjoyed, Gary enjoyed playing with his son, and it allowed Gary and I to conclude our discussion.

A few years after that, Gary would visit Laurie and Todd in the hospital following an accident when a driver crossed the middle line and crashed into their car causing serious injuries to Gary's wife and younger son, and he would have someone bring Brian to the hospital every day to have breakfast with him.

I asked older son Brian and his wife, Sally, and Todd and his wife, Katie, about their perceptions of Gary. "Tell me about Gary as a father and father-in-law," I said. Brian began by saying.

My father was definitely a kind and caring person in professional and personal life. People would call at all hours, and he was always there for them, but he was also always there for his family.

Sally added,

Gary was always extremely patient and easygoing. He was always interested in my life.

Todd said,

He is empathetic, always thinking of someone else. What is unique to him is his patience. I don't have his patience; patience and taking care of people go together."

Katie agreed:

The patience piece rings true to me. You'd be at his house, and the phone would ring, and one of his students with autism just wanted to talk with him. This would continue, and someone else might have stopped answering the phone, but not Gary. Or someone would knock on the door who was not expected, and Gary would welcome them.

Brian spoke again:

We knew growing up how in demand he was. He would travel to Saudi Arabia, and Japan every year, London annually at least. As a kid I would sometimes participate with his students in activities during his work with his clients."

Sally recalled,

Shortly after Brian and I were married, Gary took me to London with him, where I had a close friend. The first day there before his work began, Gary took us around London on a boat tour and to see all the sights. He was always trying to make sure the people he was with were well taken care of and enjoying themselves. He was an early riser, and when we were in Chapel Hill, he always brought us coffee from Sunrise Biscuit Kitchen."

Todd said,

He would very much teach by example and rarely told us what to do. He modeled the right behaviors. I'm not as good at that. I sometimes resort to telling the children what to do."

Katie concluded,

I only know him as an adult, of course. As a host he took great pride in deciding which wine to pair with food. He enjoyed being a host. He was interested in learning what great coffee is and what makes it great; he was not necessarily interested in having it. He just enjoyed life. Gary is one of the kindest, most thoughtful people I've ever been around. He seeks to understand people, and he takes an interest in them.

Passing the Torch: Eric (right) to Gary

Kaia Mates concludes,

During Gary's career at TEACCH, he affected all the many lives— professionals, parents, and people with autism—he supported and influenced for so many years. I was lucky enough to learn from him as I worked/traveled with him all over the world and witnessed firsthand his contribution to the field of autism and to so many people whose lives he helped."

Chapter Seventeen

TEACCH in the 2020s

> Our program is thriving.
>
> Laura Klinger

Laura Klinger is either the third or fourth director of TEACCH, depending on whether we count Robert Reichler, who cofounded TEACCH with Eric in 1972 and acted as codirector with him until 1976, when Eric filled the position until his retirement in 2003. Gary succeeded Eric, and then Laura became director in 2011. It seemed appropriate to ask Laura about the current status of TEACCH since she is now in her eleventh year as director.

When Laura took over as director in 2011, she was surrounded by experienced people whom she viewed as mentors from her internship at TEACCH in 1992–1993. She asked these long-term TEACCH colleagues to help create new programs to meet current needs. Lee Marcus had been a part-time consultant since retiring three years earlier, and he took the position of director of training and created a trainer certification program until he was succeeded by Kathy Hearsey, who has transitioned TEACCH from in-person to virtual training. Janet Martin was still an autism specialist in the Chapel Hill TEACCH Clinic and helped create a new early intervention program for two-year-olds, which, according to Laura, is a combination of TEACCH and ABA practices. Laura says,

The biggest challenge when I became director was that autism rates were skyrocketing, and our state funding had decreased. When I started with TEACCH in the 1990s, the rate was 3 to 4 in 10,000, but [it] was 1 in 150 in 2010. It was probably a combination of better diagnostic testing and simply more people with ASD. Now the rate is 1 in 54.

Confronted with budgetary limitations, Laura explains that TEACCH has been addressing its challenges:

We wanted to continue serving all families without charging them, but our state budget was being reduced, the number of people requesting services was increasing, and it was simply not possible. In 2012 we joined the UNC health-care system and shifted to billing insurance for diagnostic and treatment services. We have continued to provide some services for free, such as our support groups and parent education sessions. With increased funding we were able to expand our services, including reopening the Raleigh TEACCH Center, expanding the number of clinicians, and providing free resource and referral services. We have been in a growth pattern the last few years, allowing us to see more families than we were previously able to serve under the free services model of care. Last year we served families from ninety-four of the one hundred counties in North Carolina.

The state still funds a portion of our budget, and the revenue from charging for services goes right back into the services we provide. The revenue we have received has allowed us to hire more licensed clinicians, including speech-language pathologists and occupational therapists, increase the number of diagnostic services that we provide, and expand the number of clinics across the state.

We have also expanded the types of intervention services at TEACCH. In addition to our early intervention program, we have increased our interventions for autistic people across the lifespan to address mental health challenges, including anxiety interventions for school-aged children and dialectical and behavioral therapy (DBT) services for adults.

Looking toward the future, Laura says,

We have done a great deal of strategic planning with a very clear vision and goals for the future. Our vision has remained the same across fifty years: a world where all individuals with autism and their families have access to evidence-based services in their home communities. One of our strategic goals is to expand our services for autistic adolescents and adults, including understanding more about aging with autism. We have several new research faculty at TEACCH who specialize in adult employment outcomes and adult mental-health interventions, including addressing suicidality. We are also seeking to identify families with people with ASD over fifty so we can explore what happens to these people as they grow older.

We are also exploring, "How do we involve the voices of people with autism in our work?" Toward this end we will be creating an advisory council of people with ASD and members of their families. We are also designing a peer intervention program. For the last fifty years, our goal/challenge continues to be helping people with ASD understand and participate in their environment to achieve a high quality of life.

Laura indicates another challenge is that there is a huge demand for housing for autistic adults. However, the two residential homes established by TEACCH many years ago have only had one opening in the past decade. The residential program is called the Carolina Living and Learning Center (CLLC), and the two homes are located in Pittsboro, North Carolina, on a large plot of land. There is a five-bed home established in 1990 and a ten-bed home created in 1997, according to Mary Beth Van Bourgondien, who helped start the program. She was the first director of the CLLC, and she has been honored with a building on the land called the Mary E. Van Bourgondien Training Center.

Laura explains that

> TEACCH does not have the resources to create additional residential homes, so an objective is to be a resource to advise others on setting up and maintaining residential homes. Mary Beth agrees that the goal is to create models to support autistic adults around the world.
>
> Another challenge has been continuing our professional training program during the COVID-19 pandemic. Prior to the pandemic, we provided onsite training programs across the world. We just did our first in-person training since the start of the COVID pandemic, in Texas, and it is not our intention to do any international training before 2023. We have had to pivot the way in which we train professionals, converting our three-day workshop to a completely virtual format.

In its 2020–21 annual report, TEACCH reports having trained 5,617 attendees during the previous year, having held 105 virtual events, and having worked in 42 states and 46 countries. TEACCH has 177 certified advanced trainers around the world. This does not include the thousands of people conducting autism workshops and training who themselves were trained by TEACCH trainers and who are adhering to the philosophy and principles of TEACCH.

Laura sums up the current status of TEACCH with "Our program is thriving."

Chapter Eighteen

The Legacy

TEACCH has had an impact on millions of families, and I mean 'millions.'

Joaquin Fuentes, Spain

Because of TEACCH, training and intervention delivery all over the world has changed.

Cory Shulman, Israel

Gary is undoubtedly one of the giants who shaped how we serve individuals with autism in Singapore.

Ken Poon, Singapore

The principles I've learned from TEACCH have absolutely shaped me into the educator and coach I am today.

Katie Bozarth, United States

Dr. Sasaki in Japan tried to get Eric nominated for a Nobel Prize for his work on autism; the Japanese felt so strongly about his work there.

Tom Schopler

Eric and Gary were respectful of everyone; they taught us to respect people with ASD and they helped us understand how to improve their quality of life.

Viviane de Leon, Brazil

Merriam-Webster defines "legacy" as "something… received from a… predecessor."

The legacies of Eric and Gary are permanently intertwined with each other and with the TEACCH program, which Eric founded and Gary took to levels beyond what Eric might have imagined. Eric and Gary provided leadership for hundreds of TEACCH staff as well as scores of parents of children with autism; together, through TEACCH, people all around the globe have learned that individuals with autism are different but equal to the rest of us, just as we are all different from each other.

As stated earlier, I believe the true assessment of what one has accomplished is whether something a person initiated continues when one is no longer at the helm, so let's use that lens to view the legacies of Eric, Gary, and the many people who have engaged with them in pursuit of a higher quality of life for people with autism.

Does it require much imagination to appreciate the worldwide impact of TEACCH? As Barry Prizant pointed out, there are now people utilizing TEACCH practices who don't realize that what they are doing was initiated and spread by TEACCH under the direction of Eric and Gary and now Laura Klinger.

Mary Beth Van Bourgondien says,

> I was a supervisor, and I worked closely with Gary. He has trained many of us across the world, such that his contributions continue to spread and touch the lives of many."

David Preece suggests that

> Gary and the TEACCH people should receive credit for what they have done. People tend to forget that when there is something that becomes accepted practice, someone had to have thought of it. We take traffic lights for granted, but someone must have thought of the idea. Project TEACCH is all over the UK; now it underpins everything: Structured Teaching.

David Preece

Through TEACCH Gary, Eric, and their colleagues around the world have changed the way people think about autism, the people who have ASD, and the best ways to train parents and staff. They have changed the perception of parents as clients to one of parents as partners. Eric collaborated with parents to convince the North Carolina legislature to be the first in the nation to appropriate funds in support of autism research and training. Eric and Gary changed the focus of autism professionals from the weaknesses of people with autism to their strengths.

Gary designed a replicable model for training professionals and parents how to support ASD people, and the staff of TEACCH took this model to many countries around the world. Gary built on Eric's idea of parents as partners by introducing the idea of doing training with professionals, parents, and ASD people involved as partners in the effort to support families and their children with ASD. Gary stressed and spread the idea of working with teachers in their classrooms and with their ASD students and using classroom experiences, either in-person or on video, as part of presentations about autism.

TEACCH has 177 certified trainers around the world and that figure is only one indication of the world-wide reach of the TEACCH program. In many of these locales, people trained by the certified TEACCH trainers are now carrying out their mission elsewhere, employing the TEACCH philosophy and principles they have learned. For instance, according to Joaquin Fuentes, who worked with Gary and the TEACCH program in Spain and then conducted his own training throughout Europe and Asia for many years based on TEACCH principles, "Gary helped us to support many, many people in the world, and my gratitude is gigantic." As far back as the 1980s, Theo Peeters was already responding affirmatively to requests from other countries to send the Belgium trainers who had been trained by TEACCH. And Singapore was spreading TEACCH principles throughout Asia, and. . . .

Lore Gray told me,

I want to express my gratitude for Gary out loud for all the support he gave the Rhode Island Autism Project during its inception. He was my direct link to making a dream come true and directly touching our Rhode Island community and now, through our training worldwide, a much bigger circle. The years spent in training and at the national and international conferences were invigorating and changed all who attended. Please, let Gary know that his work and his kindness lives on through all of us.

Perhaps there is an even more significant criterion than the accomplishments of TEACCH for assessing the quality of the legacy that Eric and Gary leave us; it is the character they have exhibited through the respect they have demonstrated for the people they have worked with and the respect for themselves that they have merited.

What Gary would be proud to call his most important legacy might be the patience he demonstrated with everyone and the unassuming, kind, accessible, caring, empathetic, and respectful person he was, whether it was with the representatives of the king of Saudi Arabia, a high-ranking Russian official, or a woman in another state or country at her wits' end seeking advice on how to support her young child who had been diagnosed with ASD at a time when there were few resources available.

Eric, too, was beloved by the people with ASD and their families for his caring about their lives as well as his research debunking misinformation about autism.

I've mentioned previously that Gary's idol, growing up, was Willie Mays. However, Gary and Eric's lives have not aligned with a philosophy once expressed by Mays' manager Leo Durocher (1950-1954) who has often been quoted as claiming that "Nice guys finish last." Eric and Gary are nice guys who finished first in the field of autism and first as people devoted to their families.

Some people try to stake their claim to immortality by putting their names on buildings, parks, or organizations. How long does this actually achieve the purpose of etching their names in the history of the world? Often after a number of years, their legacies fade with the passing of their contemporaries and are replaced by new names. Eventually the names of almost all of our contemporaries are lost to humanity, sometimes in a few decades, maybe, for a few, in several hundred or even thousand years. However, what we pass along to others by the behaviors we model and the deeds we perform are passed along through the generations of people who succeed us.

All one needs to do is reread the many recollections of Gary and Eric's character and their contributions to the field of autism on the previous pages to know how much of what they have accomplished is being passed along to future generations of people, who may not recall their names but who will eternally benefit from what their lives have been.

Barry Prizant adds,

So much of what they innovated is now considered essential in the growing number of autism programs.

Willie Mays and the Hat Too Small

Fans knew Willie Mays as the speedster whose cap would fly off his head as he raced around the bases or chased a flyball in the outfield. In his 1988 autobiography, Mays says that he intentionally wore a hat two sizes too small because he knew his fans wanted to see the hat fall off his head. He said that he wanted to do his part to try to get the fans who were in the stands today to want to return to the stadium tomorrow.

In this way Gary and Eric were similar to Mays: always thinking about the people they wanted to serve.

Willie Mays was unquestioningly one of the greatest players to ever set foot on a baseball diamond. One can argue whether he was the very best or just among a handful of great players. There is a statue of Mays outside the ballpark of the San Francisco Giants.

Certainly the same can be said of Eric and Gary in their field of autism as is said about Mays by baseball aficionados. You can debate whether their contributions to the field of autism are greater than others from the 1960s through to the present, but few would dispute that their contributions are among the most significant of the past half century. There are awards in their names within the TEACCH program. And there are donation funds set up with the university in each of their names. But if there were more visible recognition by the University would that not accrue to the benefit of UNC just as the San Francisco Giants polished its own image by recognizing perhaps its greatest ball player?

To coincide with its 50th anniversary, what about a plaque in a highly visible location celebrating the contributions of the dedicated people who have worked for TEACCH between 1972 and the present and who are responsible for improving the quality of life for people with autism and their families - through a program developed at the University of North Carolina? And would it be overstating their contributions to the field of autism to also have statues of Eric and Gary?

Cory Shulman wrote to me that

> Gary has had an amazing effect on so many professionals, so many individuals with autism and their families, but also on our understanding of autism. He is still an inspiration to me after all these years. I have been in Israel in the field of autism since 1978. Your brother is such a special person and deserves everything you can do to make that known!

Kelly Trier said in May 2022,

> Now that I have announced my retirement, people come up to me and say how much of an impact I have had on their lives. The

strategies developed by TEACCH and what they have learned from me are the things that are brought up the most.

The majority of what I have learned in the last thirty-seven years I owe to my affiliation with the staff at Chapel Hill. Yes, there are other strategies that I use and recommend to others, but the strategies from TEACCH are the ones that have made the largest impact on my life and the lives of the thousands of kids and staff that I have had the opportunity to work with since 1985. I have been to Chapel Hill for summer training approximately fourteen times, usually for two weeks each time, the last eight to ten times as a trainer for TEACCH.

I would not have been able to do any of this without the work of Gary Mesibov and Kathy Hearsey. Those two have had a profound impact on my career. Thank you both for giving me the confidence in my beliefs and for all that you have done to make the world a better place for people with autism spectrum disorder.

Kathy and Gary, I am sure, would acknowledge that they have built upon the foundation laid by Eric Schopler and many of the people with whom they worked over the years at TEACCH.

When Marie Howley reflects on her experiences with Gary, she says,

Looking back on my teaching career since 1990, Gary was there at every stage as a mentor, colleague, and friend. He has had the greatest influence upon my work with autistic children and young people and with families. I learned so much from him and feel privileged to have had the many opportunities which he so willingly gave.

I like to think I've made a difference for people with autism and their families and that this was made possible by the ongoing support and friendship from Gary. He is a true pioneer in the field of autism around the world and has touched the lives of countless people; I am blessed to have been one of those people and am so thankful for that.

As I conclude this tribute to Eric, Gary, and so many others who have devoted their lives to providing a quality of life for people with autism, including but beyond the eighty-three people with whom I have had the privilege to speak, I hope this book will contribute to a wider understanding that people with ASD are different from the rest of us just as we are different from each other.

To repeat what Matthew Hardie said, "I'm OK; it's the rest of the world that has a problem." Hopefully after publication of this book, there will be a few more people in this world who will understand that Matthew, David Moser, and so many others diagnosed with ASD simply think differently, just as I think differently than you, the reader. Or hadn't you noticed?

On a personal note, to repeat what my childhood idol, Jackie Robinson, once said: "A life is not important except in the impact it has on other lives."

Gary, by this standard, your life, and the lives of Eric Schopler, and all of your colleagues over the years, have been important. What more could any individual do to contribute to our society? Your accomplishments are exceeded only by the unassuming manner in which you have lived your life and supported so many others in their efforts to find happiness.

Gary, I love you!

Chapter Nineteen

Come Touch His Cheek

This child of mine you stare at so,
Please come closer so you will know
Just who my child is and what I see
when those sweet eyes stare back at me

I see no limits to my child's life
Although I know
It will be filled with strife,
I'm hoping that doors will open each day
I'm praying that kindness
will come his way

You look frightened?
You tremble with fear?
Come, come closer
touch him my dear

Touch his cheek so soft
so sweet
Be one of those people
he needs to meet

Someone who will look
and hopefully see
The skill, the talent
The ability

Please come closer
You don't have to speak
Come a little closer
Just touch his cheek

And when you do
you will see
He is no different
than you or me

(Gary Shulman, MS Ed., July 2013)

Acknowledgements

Terry Arnold

Terry passed away in 2004. Along with his wife, Eileen, who continues to work in their respective fields, Terry and others referenced throughout this book, are responsible for pioneering work in the field of autism that has made England among the leading countries in Europe to provide support services for people with ASD and their families.

Laurie Mesibov

Gary's wife and equal partner in life, Laurie pursued her own career independent of Gary's while each supported the other. Laurie was one of three people to establish the Ombuds Office for the University of North Carolina in 2005. She continued in her position as the ombudsperson for UNC until her untimely death from brain cancer in 2021. Laurie and Gary were each loved and admired for their work in their respective fields and their commitment to their family.

Susan Mesibov

My wife and partner, Susan, who edited every chapter of this book and provided me the time and space to communicate with the wonderful people who have contributed their efforts and expertise to make this book truly unique in the field of autism. Susan's background as a special-education teacher for thirty years afforded her the ability to provide expertise in editing that went well beyond looking for punctuation and grammatical errors.

Eighty-three people who each spent more than an hour on Zoom with me to discuss their personal experiences with autism, many of whom followed up with information, data, and words of encouragement as I labored through the writing process. Their names and backgrounds are listed in appendix A.

My Family

Our son, Darren; daughters, Marli and Raina; daughter-in-law, Molly; nephews, Brian and Todd; their spouses, Sally and Katie; and members of our extended family whose lives on a daily basis model the values of human dignity and equality that have personified Gary's life. Each of the aforementioned people does Gary and me proud through the way they conduct themselves in their personal lives.

When one's family has health, happiness, and is socially productive, the mind is free to focus.

Definitions of Terms

ASD: Autism spectrum disorder.

autism: A complex neurological and developmental disorder that affects how a person acts, communicates, learns, and interacts with others (National Institute of Mental Health). "Autism is when your brain works differently from most other people's" (Avery Mesibov, age nine).

Structured Teaching: "Structure" within the TEACCH program refers to the active organization and direction of the physical environment and sequence of activities. Structure is essential to the functioning of individuals with autism spectrum disorder (ASD) because of their major difficulties with conceptual and organizational skills (Mesibov, Shea, and Schopler 2005). Physical structure, schedules, work systems, and visual structure combine to provide structure that is tailored to the individual. (Preece and Howley 2003). The components of Structured Teaching are the principles of TEACCH. As defined by Marie Howley, England, these are:

1. Ongoing assessment of needs to develop individualized interventions
2. Developing independence through meaningful teaching and learning
3. Building on strengths and interests of students with autism

4. Making use of visual strengths by providing individualized visual structure

5. Involving parents as coeducators (Croatia, Cypress, Macedonia, Poland, Spain)

TEACCH: Treatment and Education of Autistic and Related Communication Handicapped Children. Established in 1972 by Eric Schopler and Robert Reichler, TEACCH is an evidence-based service, training, and research program for individuals of all ages and skill levels with autism spectrum disorder.

Appendix A

Each of these people spoke at length with the author, most via Zoom, to discuss their experiences with Gary, Eric, TEACCH, or some aspect of autism. The abbreviation "FE" indicates the year they first became acquainted with autism.

Eileen Arnold: Northamptonshire, United Kingdom; autism-specialist speech-language therapist; wife of Terry Arnold, who, along with Eileen, was a pioneer in the field of autism. Terry died unexpectedly in 2004, and Eileen has carried on their work. FE 1964.

Maureen Bennie: Calgary, Alberta, Canada; founder/director of Autism Awareness Centre Inc.; parent of an autistic adult son and daughter. FE Feb 10, 1997 (her son's birth).

Joanie Berry: North Carolina; TEACCH employee for twenty-five years; secretary to Gary Mesibov 1995–2010. FE 1985.

Kelli Bielang: Kalamazoo County, Michigan; TEACCH certified advanced consultant; engagement specialist. FE 1988 (a relative).

Katie Bozarth: Washington, DC; TEACCH certified practitioner; instructional support teacher. FE 2000.

Samantha Brassington: Perth, Australia; special needs educator/leader and TEACCH certified practitioner. FE 2000.

Sloane Burgess: Ohio; Kent State University assistant professor in speech pathology, audiology, and special education; coordinator and advisor for graduate ASD certificate program and undergraduate ASD minor. FE 1988.

Mike Chapman: North Carolina; director of TEACCH employment services. FE 1988.

Christina Corsello: North Carolina; UNC TEACCH director of clinical services.

Catherine Davies: Indiana; educational consultant; TEACCH certified advanced consultant. FE 1987.

Viviane de Leon: Brazil; occupational therapist; TEACCH certified advanced consultant; FE 1988.

Dennis Debbaudt: Port Lucie, Florida; managing partner, Debbaudt Legacy Productions, LLC. FE 1980s.

Jayson Delisle: North Carolina; TEACCH employment services coordinator 1994–present.

Heather Delisle: North Carolina; wife of Jayson; acquaintance of Gary.

Grayson Delisle: North Carolina; twelve-year-old son of Jayson and Heather.

Brenda Denzler: North Carolina; mother; writer/editor/fundraiser. FE her son from about age three.

Bernadette "Det" Dekeukeleire: Remedial teacher; cofounder, Flemish Autism Association (1985); coordinator, *sterkmakers in autisme* (strong makers in autism), a Belgian center supporting autism awareness and autism friendliness; wife of Peter Vermeulen.

John Donvan: Multiple Emmy-award winning correspondent for ABC and bestselling coauthor of *A Different Key* (2016).

Lawrence Dubin: Michigan; emeritus professor of law, University of Detroit Mercy; coauthor of *Caught in the Web of the Criminal Justice System: Autism, Developmental Disabilities, and Sex Offenses*. FE 2003 (Larry's son, born in 1977, received the diagnosis at age 27. He was criminally charged with a non-touch sex offense.)

Katie Eyes: Daughter-in-law of Gary, wife of Todd.

Catherine Faherty: North Carolina; TEACCH teacher and psycho-educational specialist; trainer; TEACCH certified advanced consultant (retired), Carol Gray Social Story trainer; Autism Society of North Carolina direct service staff member. FE 1984.

Toni Flowers: Indiana; teacher; director of special education supervising autism programs; author; 1989 Autism Society of America Teacher of the Year. FE 1970s.

Joaquin Fuentes: San Sebastian, Spain; GAUTENA (Gipuzkoa Autism Society); medical director; research consultant. FE 1981.

Tom Galperin: Ohio; autism consultant; TEACCH certified practitioner; TEACCH supported employment coach (1996–2005). FE 1996 in North Carolina.

Lore L. Gray: Rhode Island; teacher; trainer; consultant; adult program facilitator; cofounder of the Rhode Island Autism Project. FE 1968 as a volunteer.

Tomoko R. Haramaki: Japan; president of the Japanese TEACCH certified professionals' network; TEACCH certified advanced consultant. FE 1979.

Anne Haeussler: Germany; autism specialist; TEACCH certified advanced consultant and trainer; intern/fellow at Asheville TEACCH Center (1990–92). FE 1987.

Annette Hardie: England; civil servant; school governor; family support worker; nursery worker.

Ian Hardie: England; retired quality steel engineer.

Matthew Hardie: England; central service support manager at an office that does work involving business assurance and business governance. Matthew is thirty-five and is a person with autism

Kathy Hearsey: North Carolina; educator; current director of training at TEACCH. FE 1978 as a volunteer in the TEACCH classroom at the hospital.

Marie Howley: England; autism specialist; teacher; university senior lecturer. FE 1982.

Kara Hume: Arizona and North Carolina; TEACCH certified advanced consultant; associate professor in the School of Education at UNC at Chapel Hill. FE 1990.

Steve Hutton: North Carolina; database manager/statistical programmer for North Carolina's participation in the CDC's national surveillance of autism prevalence and related research (2006–2010); employee grievance support.

Sussanne Hvidfeldt: Denmark; Langagerskolen (special-education school) consultant. FE 1985 as a teacher.

Lori Ireland: One of the founders of EV (Extraordinary Adventures), which provides employment for people with IDD along with their typically developing peers; parent of a child with autism.

Birgitta Karlsson: Sweden; Metodutvecklare educator, supervisor. FE 1998.

Laura Grofer Klinger, PhD: TEACCH executive director since 2010; associate professor, UNC School of Medicine, Department of Psychiatry. FE 1981 (volunteered at a school for autistic adolescents during freshman year at Stanford University).

Steve Kroupa: North Carolina and Japan; clinical child/pediatric psychologist; former clinical director, Fayetteville TEACCH Center; emeritus professor, UNC at Chapel Hill School of Medicine. FE 1987.

Louise Loosen: Western Australia; special needs teacher. FE 1998.

Catherine "Cathy" Lord, PhD: George Tarjan Distinguished Professor of Psychiatry and Education, UCLA. FE 1969.

Steven R. Love: North Carolina; former clinical director, Asheville TEACCH Center; licensed psychologist with Olson Huff Center for Child Development (ten years). FE 1987.

Keith Lovett: England; director, *Autism Independent UK* (SFTAH); father of a son with autism. Keith first worked with Gary in 1987. FE 1985.

Lee Marcus: North Carolina; clinical director, Chapel Hill TEACCH Center (retired). FE 1973.

Kaia Mates: North Carolina; TEACCH autism specialist. FE 1979.

Anne McGuire: North Carolina; TEACCH autism specialist; educational coach for the Eastern Band of the Cherokee Indians Head Start Program. FE 1977.

Gary Mesibov: Educational consultant; former director of TEACCH.

Brian Mesibov: Charlotte, North Carolina; older son of Gary and Laurie Mesibov, attorney / law-firm partner.

Sally Mesibov: Daughter-in-law of Gary, wife of Brian.

Todd Mesibov: Younger son of Gary and Laurie; attorney/administrator, Duke University.

Avery Mesibov: Granddaughter of Susan and Don Mesibov.

Marli Mesibov: Boston, Massachusetts; content strategist and feminist; daughter of Susan and Don Mesibov.

Raina Mesibov: Raina is manager of two Ben & Jerry's stores in Cambridge, Massachusetts and she has been a Technical Advisor for this book.

Susan Mesibov: Teacher of special education (thirty years); supervisor of student teachers and teacher of a class on inclusion at St. Lawrence University (fourteen years). Susan provided editorial support on this manuscript.

Susan Moreno: Founder and CEO of MAAP Services for Autism; author; lecturer; parent of child with ASD. FE 1975 when daughter was diagnosed at age two.

David Shannon Moser: Person with ASD; accounting technician, UNC TEACCH. David wants us to know that "I live independently in my own townhouse in Chapel Hill, have my own car, and I drive to my job at TEACCH, where I work full time with full benefits." David is a graduate of UNC, class of 1989, and "I have a double-major BA in Geography and Political Science from UNC Chapel Hill. Go Heels!"

Signe Naftel graduated Emory University, 2002; School Psychology Doctoral work at UNC, 2002-2007; working for TEACCH since 2003; developed an on-line curriculum for autistic adults to find and keep a job. FE 2001

Brigitte Cartier-Nelles: Psychologist and TEACCH certified advanced consultant; trainer and consultant in autism in France and the French-speaking part of Switzerland. FE 1985, a nonverbal adolescent.

Vaya Papageorgiou: Thessaloniki, Greece; child and adolescent psychiatrist; autism specialist; former intern at Asheville TEACCH Center (1997). FE 1994.

Joanne C. Phillips: Arizona; president of consulting and staff development firm Arizona Education Cadre; Arizona state director of exceptional student services (retired).

Nathalie Plante: Canada; special education at University of Québec in Montréal; TEACCH® certified advanced consultant. FE 1983.

Ken Poon: Singapore; associate professor, Nanyang Technological University; President, Rainbow Centre. FE 1996.

Cathy Pratt: Indiana; director, Indiana Resource Center for Autism, Indiana Institute om Disability and Community, Indiana University. FE fifty-plus years ago at a summer camp in her hometown.

David Preece: England; service manager, residential and community services; associate professor in autism, University of Northampton. FE 1979.

Barry M. Prizant: Cranston, Rhode Island; visiting scholar/adjunct professor, Artists and Scientists as Partners Program, Brown University; director, Childhood Communication Services. FE 1968 as a residential summer-camp counselor.

Joanne G. Quinn: Rhode Island; executive director, The Autism Project (in her twentieth year); parent of a child with autism.

Christina Rukki: Cover design advisor.

Betsy Schopler, first wife f Eric Schopler, 1953-1970

Robert Schopler: Eric and Betsy's second child.

Tom Schopler: Eric and Betsy's youngest child.

Susie Schopler: Eric and Betsy's oldest child.

Victoria Shea: TEACCH trainer; coauthor with Eric Schopler and Gary Mesibov of *The TEACCH Approach to Autism Spectrum Disorders* (2005).

Kayoko (Kay) Shigematsu: Japan; conference interpreter (English–Japanese).

Andy Short: Clinical psychologist; part-time TEACCH faculty,. FE 1969.

Cory Shulman: Head of the Autism Center, Hebrew University of Jerusalem. FE 1968.

Gary Shulman: New York City; director, Special Needs Consulting and Training (retired); program director of social services, Resources for Children with Special Needs, Inc.

Laurie Sperry: Colorado; director and founder, Autism Forensics and Criminal Investigation Clinic, Autism Services and Programs. FE 1980.

Melissa Sreckovic: North Carolina and Michigan; associate professor, Education Department, University of Michigan–Flint. FE 2008.

Svanhildur "Svany" Svavarsdottir: Iceland; special-education speech-language pathologist; TEACCH advanced certified consultant; grandmother of four autistic children. FE 1973.

Kyoko Tanaka: Japan, child psychiatrist/pediatrician, National Hospital Organization, Kikuchi Hospital; sibling of a person with ASD. FE 1998.

Regnar H. Thisted: Denmark; consultant, Langagerskolen special-education school. FE 1981 as a teacher.

Fukuda Toshiyuki: Japan; reporter and photographer. FE 1980.

Jen Townsend: Wisconsin; educational consultant, Universal Access Consulting, LLC; Graduate Certification for Education of Individuals with Autism. FE 1998 as a peer learning assistant in Maryland.

Kelly Trier: Cedar Rapids, Iowa; TEACCH certified advanced-level trainer; autism consultant (retired). FE 1985.

Tokio Uchiyama, DMSc: Professor, Fukushima College, Japan; president, TEACCH Society of Japan; TEACCH certified advanced consultant. FE 1986 as a child psychiatrist.

Mary E. Van Bourgondien: TEACCH faculty member; former clinical director, Chapel Hill TEACCH; professor, UNC at Chapel Hill. FE 1970s.

Peter Vermeulen: researcher; lecturer; and trainer; author of more than fifteen books about autism; husband of Bernadette Dekeukeleire. Peter started his career at the Flemish Autism Association in 1987.

Linda R. Watson: Former TEACCH research associate; professor of speech and hearing sciences, providing clinical services, conducting autism research, and preparing future SLPs and researchers to work with the autistic population. FE 1960s via volunteer work and babysitting.

Alice Wertheimer: North Carolina; TEACCH visitor coordinator; TEACCH conference coordinator (1992–2009); parent. FE 1989 with David's diagnosis at age three.

Alexander Westphal: New Haven, Connecticut; associate professor of psychiatry, Yale University. FE his grandmother had a school for kids with autism, and he had an uncle with autism.

Appendix B

The following are excerpts from an email from David Moser to the author on June 17, 2022, a few months after a two-hour Zoom to discuss his life as a high-performing person with ASD:

Hi Don,

I hope that things are going well for you and your family and for Gary and his family too. I really do miss him a lot as time goes on. He means a lot to me as a TEACCH client on the autism spectrum. He was a friend of mine and my parents and a mentor from whom I learned many things about work, life, friends, and family and being comfortable with whom I am today.

Gary gave me great advice about how to interact with others around me, including many of our mutual colleagues and friends both on and off the autism spectrum, several of whom I have great relationships with today, in part due to Gary breaking the ice and introducing us. He was a great listener with thoughtful and helpful advice and a great conversationalist and storyteller with a dry and wry sense of humor too. I really do miss him now with all that has transpired since we last saw each other at a dinner with our social group supper club in late spring/early summer of 2019, three years ago.

Stay well and cool this summer, too, and have a great Father's Day weekend, too, Don. Go Heels! ☺

Best Regards,
David Moser

Appendix C

Laurie Mesibov

The following is in tribute to Laurie Mesibov, the equal partner to Gary Mesibov, excerpted from her obituary with edits by the author:

Laurie Mesibov, January 28, 1946–March 31, 2021.

Chapel Hill, North Carolina—Laurie Mesibov, seventy-five, of Chapel Hill, passed away on March 31, 2021, after a hard-fought nineteen-month battle with glioblastoma, a highly aggressive brain cancer.

Laurie was born January 28, 1946, in Boston, Massachusetts, to Stanley and Eleanor Levenson. She attended Stanford University in Palo Alto, California, and graduated with her BA in 1967.

During her study-abroad program at Stanford in Paris, Laurie met the love of her life, Gary, and they were married the summer after graduation in August 1967. They lived on Guam for three years, where Laurie taught fourth grade, and ultimately settled in Chapel Hill in 1973. They raised two sons, Brian, and Todd, both attorneys. Once both children were in school full time, Laurie chose to go back to school herself, attending the UNC School of Law beginning in the fall of 1980.

During law school she provided one of the greatest examples of her dedication and persistence. Shortly after the first semester of her already challenging 1L year, Laurie suffered two broken arms after being hit head-on in a car accident. Her son, Todd, was also seriously injured. While that would have stopped most people, Laurie was undeterred. Laurie took a short leave to recover and care for her children and then returned to law school to earn her JD in 1984.

After graduating from law school, Laurie devoted her thirty-five-year career to the University of North Carolina. She was a long-time faculty member in the School (formerly Institute) of Government, where she specialized in public-school law. She worked in the Office of the Provost from 1996–2000, chaired the Performance Management Review Board, served as an advisor to SPA grievance panels, and was a member of the Faculty Grievance Committee, Faculty Executive Committee, and Faculty Council. When UNC opened an ombuds office in 2005 to address a need for conflict and dispute resolution within the university, Laurie was the first faculty ombudsperson, and she remained in that role for the rest of her career.

Throughout her years at Carolina, Laurie served as a valued confidant, advisor, mentor, counselor, friend, and—the role she enjoyed most—champion for others.

"Laurie strongly believed that law and compassion were

compatible," said Dean Mike Smith. "She worked in the field of school law, and over the years, school officials and their attorneys relied on her for first-rate legal analysis. They were devoted to Laurie. They relied on her judgment, wisdom, and common sense—and for her willingness to engage them in challenging and sometimes uncomfortable conversations. Laurie meant a great deal to me, and she meant a great deal to the School."

Laurie loved swimming laps at the UNC faculty/staff pool, making it her goal each summer to swim the number of laps equal to her age. She capped the goal at one mile, which she impressively achieved at age seventy-three shortly before becoming sick in 2019. Each year Laurie invited new members of the community—friends and strangers—to join other friends and family at her house for Thanksgiving dinner, often including people with autism, many of whom had never been to a house other than their own for a meal.

Laurie is survived by her husband, Gary; sister, Toby; sons, Brian and Todd; daughters-in-law, Sally and Kate; and her beloved grandchildren, Anna, Claire, Eleanor and Milo.

Made in the USA
Monee, IL
30 September 2024

66209225R00174